Walls to Bridges:
The Global Ethic

Hans Küng

Contributions by
Günther Gebhardt and Stephan Schlensog

Tribute by
Leonard Swidler

—Revised Edition IIb—

Published by iPub Global Connection, LLC
1050 W. Nido Avenue, Mesa, AZ 85210
www.iPubCloud.com
Email: info@iPubCloud.com
US telephone: 484-775-0008

Walls to Bridges: The Global Ethic
ISBN: 978-1-948575-33-1
Library of Congress Control Number: 2020936940
https://lccn.loc.gov/2020936940

Also available as an eBook. *https://ipubcloud.com/marketplace/walls-to-bridges-the-global-ethic/*

Cover Design by Arewa Abiodun Ibrahim
Cover Image by Shutterstock/Arthimedes

Praise for Walls to Bridges

"The Parliament of the World's Religions highly recommends this book, which promises to bring the Global Ethic—the Parliament's signature document—to a wider audience. The Global Ethic, written in part by Professor Hans Küng at the behest of the Parliament and with contributions from Parliament leaders Dr. Thomas Baima and Dr. Daniel Gómez-Ibáñez, is the product of months of consultation with several hundred religious leaders and scholars from many of the world's religions and regions. Ratified by the Parliament's Board of Trustees in 1993 and again in 2018, when it was expanded, it has been endorsed by thousands attending the Parliament's international convenings in 1993 (Chicago) and in 2018 (Toronto). An expression of the basic ethical commitments shared by people throughout the world, religious or not, the Global Ethic was intended from the start to remain a living document. The Handbook produced by Küng and his Global Ethic Foundation provides valuable resources to support ongoing conversations about the Global Ethic. It will, no doubt, prove helpful to individuals and groups as they engage the Global Ethic's moral directives and consider how best to put them into practice."
Myriam Renaud, Ph.D., Principal Investigator and Project Director of the Global Ethic Project, Parliament of the World's Religions

"Based on the seminal work of renowned scholar Hans Küng's *Global Responsibility: In Search of a New World Ethic, Walls to Bridges* is "a book written for our times." The rise of the Far Right with its anti-immigrant agendas, anti-Semitism, and Islamophobia in increasingly multiethnic, multireligious, and multicultural societies have created a crisis that threatens domestic stability and

global peace. The *Walls to Bridges* provides a shared strategy and response, based on fundamental democratic and ethical values and attitudes, for the acceptance of diversity and pluralism."
John L. Esposito, University Professor of Religion and International Affairs, Georgetown University

"A concise updated manual of Professor Hans Küng's trailblazing recommendation for a global ethic based on commonalities yet preserving diverse ethical perspectives. One of Hans Küng's great contributions to the common wellbeing of humanity is this revised and updated *Walls to Bridges*, without threatening the diverse heritages of the world's manifold cultures."
Paul Mojzes, Professor Emeritus of Religious Studies, Rosemont College

"The global ethic is a powerful idea for discussion and debate. It focuses people from a range of identities on what it means to build bridges for the common good. Bravo for bringing this back to the center of public conversation."
Eboo Patel, Founder and President Interfaith Youth Core and Editor of "Interreligious/Interfaith Studies: Defining a Field"

"There are moments of hope in difficult times, and slivers of light in dark ones. All it takes is to listen to that voice inside ourselves that realizes and respects our humanity, and in that process, realizes and respects that elemental, beautiful, fragile, and courageous humanity in others. The decades-long work to fashion the terms for a global ethic continues to provide both a personal and globally shared resource for this hope and light. In a time when our political fears and religious suspicions are building momentum for building walls, those ethics that we share as human and embodied creatures provide a counter-narrative for collaboration and possibility. This handbook poetically conjures the urgency for discovering the ethical values that are not only deeply rooted in one's personal experience or cultural memory, but also shared by others who on the surface seem so different or distant. *Walls to Bridges* speak interiorly to every individual, yet is inherently inclusive for recognizing the moral and imaginative qualities we share as human beings. As we are experiencing, the earth's political, economic, and environmental challenges are deeply interconnected. More and more, we need to develop capacities for shared solutions to shared problems. *Walls to Bridges* provides the moral and ethical foundation for this much needed, and mutually hopeful, collaboration."

John Dalla Costa, Founding Director of the Centre for Ethical Orientation

"Professor Leonard Swidler, President of the Dialogue Institute at Temple University, and Hans Küng, President of the Foundation for a Global Ethic, have worked for years with enormous dedication toward achieving an urgently needed global ethic. Similar appeals have been made by His Holiness the Dalai Lama (*Beyond Religion: Ethics for a Whole World*), Sharif Abdullah (*Creating a World That Works for All*), and such visionaries as Teilhard de Chardin, Matthew Fox, and Barbara Marx Hubbard. These brilliant, compassionate, creative thinkers invite and encourage us to bring open minds and hearts to each other, in order to establish deeper understanding and respect across religious, ethnic, political, and gender lines.

Seeking to attain a wise balance between honoring individuality and establishing necessary rules for humanity, *Walls to Bridges* poses the right questions for deep contemplation and effective action. The guidelines given inspire healthy, authentic dialogue among groups, and offer opportunities to dive more deeply into universal answers for today's urgent challenges.

Those of us involved in interfaith work are grateful for every opportunity to be guided to incisive questioning and to bring creative focus on healthy solutions that may ease tensions, expand understanding, and honor unity in diversity."
Rev. Dr. Maxine Kaye, Spiritual Leader Greater Philadelphia Center for Spiritual Living

"Very highly recommended! Our global age has emerged with global challenges: the climate crisis, widespread economic inequality, and the resurgence of anti-democratic forms of governance, among many others. Addressing these issues requires transdisciplinary work at the level of the problem, an approach that is truly global in both its planetary-scale and comprehensive perspective. Enter *Walls to Bridges*—an ambitious and thoughtful guide providing a historical and conceptual overview of the "global ethic" approach to addressing our many modern crises, as well as offering suggestions for how this timely project can be implemented. And for those of us working at the vanguard of new religious thought, it is especially heartening to see the handbook's innovative engagement with the transformative potential of religion and spirituality."
Gregory Hansell, Executive Director, Omega Center

Welcome Home to iPubCloud.com

Welcome to iPub Global Connection! You've selected a book from our international library that focusses on transformative materials from authors all over the world. You might be a scholar, an avid reader, a parent, a teacher, or a student, seeking empowerment or world sustainability.

We are committed to your contributions to a better world. Often, we doubt that alone, we have the ability or opportunity to make any real impact. When that thought comes up, just say, "backspace, delete." Together, we *will* influence the world, causing crucial changes to ensure a habitable world for future generations.

Join with change agents all over the world to listen to *their* ideas, share *your* ideas, and support creating and protecting the world for your great-great-grandchildren.

How would *you* begin to define how we could connect as global citizens? One way is to be open to learn and understand other cultures and peoples with whom we can connect through dialogue. Other ways include music, art, blogs, podcasts…all to help younger generations learn to live as global citizens and enjoy the global community.

iPubCloud.com is working to help achieve these transformations. Together, we can be guides towards world peace and improving communication through dialogue. Our international writers, authors, thinkers, and scholars are here to make you think….

CONTENTS

Tribute to Hans Küng
by Leonard Swidler

Dear Hans,

It's been a half a century (1959) since we first contacted each other at the University of Tübingen, Germany! What a whirlwind of profound, world-changing activity you have engaged in throughout these fifty years!

Congratulations on this occasion of the English language publication of your latest book, *Walls to Bridges* (original: *Handbuch Weltethos*) and your continued spreading of the movement for a Global Ethic started over a quarter-century ago.

Yes, your leadership of this movement led to the realization that there are, in fact, certain basic ethical principles that have been affirmed by all the significant ethical and religious systems of the world.

Your support of the world-foundational Global Ethic has led to the awareness it is not a static principle, but dynamic. Two or three centuries ago, most of the world's ethical systems assumed human slavery was acceptable. Today, that assumption is gone. While slavery still exists, no living religious or ethical system would today defend it.

Other ethical principles are moving in the same expansive manner. To mention two on a similar path moving toward universal acceptance:

- the equality of women and men (not sameness) and
- the ethical treatment of the global ecology

Your book, *Walls to Bridges*, builds upon worldwide shared ethical principles. You challenge us in our various disciplines, both individually and in our work worlds (business, politics, communications, and medicine, et al.) to integrate these fundamental Global Ethic principles into an expanding and deepening practice.

Your work is a bridge to make the Global Ethic real in our lives and those of all our neighbors and associates here and across the world. We thank you, Hans, for your wisdom; you're leading the way and inspiring us!

Your friend,

Leonard Swidler

Preface
A Vision for the Future

Amidst the momentous upheavals of the years 1989/90, no one could have foretold what would happen to a slim book with its ambitious title "Projekt Weltethos" (engl. "Global Responsibility. In Search of a New World Ethic"). The Swiss newspaper *Neue Zürcher Zeitung* wrote at the time: "In a time of never-ending wars, of new and bloody racial tensions–it is more topical than ever: a unified world needs a unified ethic; while a global society does not need a single uniform religion or ideology, it does need certain unifying standards, values, ideals, and goals... This slim, densely written book is a resoundingly powerful address, not far from prophetic gesture..."

The agenda was clear right from the start and the message has continued to become even clearer and more tangible in the quarter-century that has since passed:

"No peace among nations without peace between religions. No peace between religions without a dialogue between religions. No dialogue between religions without shared ethical values and standards."

From the start, the sentences listed above also included the sentence: "No dialogue between religions without basic research into religions." This sentence was also the motto of the book *Judaism*, initially published in 1991 in German as the first volume of a trilogy *The Religious Situation of Our Time* and sponsored by the Robert Bosch Jubilee Foundation and the Daimler-Benz Fund. Together with subsequent publications (cf. Bibliography), without which the Global Ethic Project would have been unthinkable, it was a testimony of intensive theological, philosophical, and religious research.

The Global Ethic Project's charter and founding document was the "Declaration Toward a Global Ethic" issued by the Parliament of the World's Religions in Chicago on September 4, 1993. This Declaration clearly formulates the principles and directives of a global ethic based on the great religious and ethical traditions of humanity and restated for our modern times.

– The two basic principles:

1. The *Principle of Humanity*: "Every human being must be treated humanely and not inhumanely."

2. The *Golden Rule of Reciprocity*: "Do unto others what you would have others do unto you."
– The Five Directives or Imperatives of Humanity:

1. A culture of *nonviolence* and *respect for all life*: "You shall not kill—but you shall also not torture, torment, or hurt,"—or to put it positively, "Have respect for life!"

2. A culture of *solidarity* and a *just economic order*: "You shall not steal—but you shall also not exploit, bribe, or corrupt,"—or to state it positively, "Act honestly and fairly!"

3. A culture of *tolerance* and a life of *truthfulness*: "You shall not lie—but you shall also not deceive, falsify, manipulate,"—or to put it positively, "Speak and act truthfully!"

4. A culture of *equal rights* and *partnership between men and women*: "You shall not abuse sexuality—but you shall also not abuse, humiliate, or degrade your partner,"—or to put it positively, "Respect and love one another!"

In November 2018, on the 25th anniversary of the "Declaration Toward a Global Ethic," increasingly pressing ecological problems led to the four Directives being supplemented by a fifth one:

5. Commitment to a culture of *sustainability* and *care for the Earth*: "You shall not be greedy!" Or to put it positively: "Remember the good of all!"

At the time, many people considered the project to be purely utopian. But the idea of a global ethic is not a utopia; it is not a place of nowhere; it is a *vision*: it shows how a world, perhaps not an ideal world but certainly a better world, could and can look. It is a vision *for the future*: we and all people who work together towards this end are convinced that a commitment to promoting respect and understanding between cultures and a commitment to promoting ethical standards in society, in politics and the economy, in learning and education is desperately necessary. And a global ethic is a *realistic* vision, a vision which can naturally not be achieved overnight but will take time. That vision has already been applied to the topical social questions of thirty or forty years ago: a new understanding of peace and disarmament, an awakening sensitivity to environmental problems, and a new view of the roles of men and women based on partnership. All of these issues had ethical dimensions and the process of rethinking and revising our ideas has taken decades—and has not yet been concluded.

The Global Ethic Project came a long way in its first two decades. To provide an overview and introduction, the most important milestones of the Project are briefly outlined below:

1989 February: UNESCO symposium, Paris: "No Global Peace without Religious Peace"
1989 November: fall of the Berlin Wall
1990 February: World Economic Forum, Davos: "Why we need global ethical standards to survive"
1990 May: "Projekt Weltethos" (engl. "Global Responsibility" 1991)
1993 Chicago: Parliament of the World's Religions: "Declaration Toward a Global Ethic"
1995 Establishment of the Global Ethic Foundation in Tübingen
1995 "Ja zum Weltethos" (engl. "Yes to a Global Ethic" 1996)
1997 Update and continuation of the book "Projekt Weltethos": "Weltethos für Weltpolitik und Weltwirtschaft" (engl. "A Global Ethic for Global Politics and Economics" 1997)
1997 InterAction Council of Former Heads of State and Government proposes a "Universal Declaration of Human Responsibilities"
1998 Kuala Lumpur: International Confederation of Stock Exchanges "Ethical Standards for International Financial Transactions"
1998 "Wissenschaft und Weltethos" [Science and a Global Ethic] with essays on business ethics and law, political and educational

science, natural science and ethics

2001 Baden-Baden: interdisciplinary symposium on "Globale Unternehmen—Globales Ethos. Der globale Markt erfordert neue Standards und eine globale Rahmenordnung" [Global Companies—A Global Ethic: A global market demands new standards and a global framework]

2001 United Nations: report by a "Group of Eminent Persons" with the title "Crossing the Divide. Dialogue among Civilizations, Report for the United Nations" available online at: www.un.org

2002 Tübingen: interdisciplinary symposium "Ein neues Paradigma internationaler Beziehungen? Ethische Herausforderungen für die Gestaltung der Weltpolitik" [A New Paradigm for International Relations? Ethical challenges in the shaping of global policies], published in: "Friedenspolitik. Ethische Grundlagen internationaler Beziehungen" (2003) [Peace Policies. The Ethical Basis of International Relations]

2004 Conclusion of the trilogy on the current religious situation with the volume "Islam. Geschichte, Gegenwart, Zukunft" (engl. "Islam: Past, Present & Future" 2007)

2009 New York/Basel: manifesto "Global Economic Ethic"

2011 Establishment of the Global Ethic Institute at the University of Tübingen

2011 October, Berlin: world premiere of the composition 'Weltethos' by Jonathan Harvey played by the Berlin Philharmonic (Sir Simon Rattle)

2011 November, Washington, Georgetown University: international symposium on "Global Ethic, Law and Policy"

2012 April, Tübingen: opening of the Global Ethic Institute - lectures and seminars commence

2012 October, Birmingham: premiere of the English version of the composition 'Weltethos' played by the City of Birmingham Symphony Orchestra (Edward Gardner)

2013 April, Tübingen: The presidency of the Global Ethic

Foundation was handed over to Eberhard Stilz, former president of the Constitutional Court of Baden-Württemberg

As its founding president, I am very pleased that after the baton passed to my successor, the activities of the Global Ethic Foundation have been continued so dynamically and creatively. Under the motto "Living Together in Diversity," the Global Ethic Foundation is involved in many different initiatives promoting interfaith dialogue which range from local dialogue initiatives to national and international interfaith conferences to the establishment of Councils of Religions in various municipalities across the state of Baden-Württemberg. World LAB is a very successful intercultural values project which has been introduced in a number of vocational schools teaching refugees with the aim of integrating young people forced to flee their homes. Then there are also the many different initiatives to teach values, aimed primarily at educational facilities. This includes the very successful Global Ethic Schools, a designation used by the Global Ethic Foundation to certify schools which are trying to create a school culture guided by the precepts of a global ethic; the provision of many different educational media for use by daycare centers and schools; training materials for teachers and daycare center staff; projects for the prevention of violence, the prevention of radicalization and the promotion of democracy; and lastly, but not least, the wide-ranging educational work of the Global Ethic Foundation at home and abroad and the Foundation's numerous international global ethic initiatives and projects in India, Hong Kong, and elsewhere.

These milestones involved a lot of effort, and so, particularly in Part II, in various sections headed "personal background," I will be highlighting the extent of the preliminary groundwork which went into the respective subprojects. It should become clear that the Global Ethic Project did not simply appear from nowhere but is based on decades of detailed basic research, much of it already undertaken in the Institute for Ecumenical Research (1964–1996). An overview of the relevant basic literature is provided at the end of the book. Many years' experience of the development, dissemination, and practical implementation of these ideas has repeatedly confirmed their relevance and necessity.

And now a handbook: "Germans must have very big hands," an American scholar once commented with a sideways glance at the size of some handbooks. This handbook is small, but it should nevertheless provide a compact overview of ideas, their foundation, and the implementation of a global ethic today. To keep it small and portable, I have avoided including references and footnotes. The relevant references are easy to find in our various books; on the history of the concept, see also the comments by different authors in "Dokumentation zum Weltethos" [Documentation on a Global Ethic], edited by H. Küng (2002).

This small handbook served also as a guideline for the new Global Ethic Institute (WEIT) which was made possible by a very generous contribution of the Karl-Schlecht Foundation. This book is gratefully dedicated to Prof. H.C., Dipl. Ing. Karl Schlecht and his wife Brigitte, who have generously supported the Global Ethic Foundation for many years.

I am pleased and grateful that a revised English edition of this Global Ethic Handbook is now being published—revised and updated by Dr. Stephan Schlensog and Dr. Günther Gebhardt. This publication was made possible by my dear friend and fellow campaigner for a global ethic, Prof. Dr. Len Swidler (Temple University, Philadelphia), his sister Sandi Swidler Billingslea, her colleague Sandy Mayer, and the financial support of the Global

Ethic Foundation. My warmest thanks to all of you!

Tübingen, June 2019

Hans Küng

I.

What is a Global Ethic?

The Global Ethic Project strives for peace between religions, cultures, and nations based on certain jointly held fundamental ethical values, standards, and attitudes. For more than two decades, its timeliness has continually increased as has the support for the project. Indeed, the concept of a global ethic is currently—and not merely because of the global financial and economic crisis—enjoying a boom. Moreover, the misunderstandings which often occur with a new project have been ironed out for those willing to look for information themselves. The reasons and lines of argumentation, which in the first phase derived primarily from the world religions, have since been confirmed and strengthened by information from many different disciplines. Nevertheless, the project has continued to remain a living and open process up to the present day. It is a sign of its vitality that it continues to tackle—creatively, I hope—new questions arising from cultural, social, and religious developments.

1. Global ethic as an opportunity

(1) A global age requires a global ethic

People's thoughts and actions—in politics, the economy, education and training, even culture and sports—are increasingly being played out against a global horizon. For this reason, an ethical orientation which also has a global dimension is more necessary than ever. We read and hear on an almost daily basis about various crises and their moral preconditions or consequences.

One question which is often asked is which crisis is the most dangerous. My answer to that is: the most dangerous crisis is the current accumulation of global crises. We live in a time where several fundamental crises are influencing and reinforcing one another. Fukushima is a symbol of how an earthquake, a tsunami, and technical and political failure can escalate and exacerbate each other. We are seeing the emergence of climate and energy crises, financial and economic crises, debt and national crises—not only in developing countries but also in Greece, Portugal, Italy, Spain, Ireland, Great Britain, and in the USA, the leading western world power. We see these crises even in France and Germany. None of these crises are natural catastrophes–they are human-made.

There is no universal remedy that could help us resolve individual crises or all of these crises together. Of course, a global ethic cannot offer a pre-packaged solution to these problems in the sense of providing a recipe for success. But the concept of a global ethic is at least an effective attempt at finding answers as it offers an ethical frame of reference (globally and domestically) and a moral compass during the crises of our globalized world which may be helpful in all areas of life, in matters big and small, to both young and old.

(2) A global ethic for crisis prevention

Natural disasters cannot be prevented; catastrophes caused by human beings can. In the introduction to my book *Global Responsibility*, I discussed three global catastrophes and three key dates when humankind would have had the opportunity to bring about a new and better world order: in 1918 (after the First World War), in 1945 (after the Second World War), and in 1989 (after the end of the Cold War between East and West).

In 1990 I voiced the widely shared hope of a new world order — which was duly promised and billed as "A New World Order" by the then President of the United States, George Bush Senior, after the first war in Iraq. But sadly, I was forced to realize after two decades that this hope of nations has clearly not materialized in any way.

That this enormous hope was disappointed was due not merely to a failure of institutions (of national governments, parliaments, and international organizations), but also to a catastrophic moral failure. Most of the catastrophes could have been avoided with fair, honest, and constructive policies:

- The emergence of the new type of international terrorism could have been avoided: just imagine if Israel had concluded a fair peace with the Arab nations immediately after winning the Six Day War in 1967 (as some perspicacious Israelis hoped)—both with Egypt and with a newly established Palestinian state.

- The war in Afghanistan could have been avoided: just imagine if, instead of waging war on land, sea, and air—a war which was highly risky from start—the superpower had undertaken efficient, internationally coordinated police operations and covert operations, as were initially considered, against the terrorist network al-Qaeda (not a state!).

- The second war in Iraq launched by President George Bush, who wished to impose American hegemony in the Middle East, could have been avoided. Just imagine if the dictator Saddam Hussein had been paralyzed by his political and military isolation and, at the same time, a fair solution to the Palestinian problem had been proposed.

- The rash expansion of the European Union could have been avoided: just imagine if efforts had been devoted not merely to constructing a financial roof based on the Euro but at the same time carrying out the internal changes to the Union agreed in the Maastricht Treaty. This would involve a reform of the Union's institutions (manner of voting, terms of accession to the EU, etc.) which could have prevented fraudulent accessions to the European Union.

- The revocation of the Stability and Growth Pact, initially by the German government, could have been avoided. Imagine if Germany, and subsequently France, had set Europe and the world an example of how to reform the rampant welfare state so that social benefits would be affordable, cutting back on super-fluous subsidies, changing unaffordable laws, stimulating the economy, and reducing unemployment.

- And finally, the international financial and economic crisis could also have been avoided. Just imagine if efforts had been directed toward creating a new financial framework, a new Bretton Woods agreement as many people demanded, and the casino capitalism of Wall Street, London, Frankfurt, and Zurich had been held in check.

All of these crises have also had an *ethical dimension*. All attempts to find solutions will fall short as long as efforts are not focused at the level of ethics, at changing the inner attitudes of the stake-holders and decision-makers, at working towards a change in attitudes, at attempting a return to responsibility and basic ethical standards.

(3) Democratic and ethical values

Values such as Freedom, Equality, and Solidarity which spread from Europe and achievements such as democracy, human rights, and tolerance would be more easily accepted globally if they were underpinned by ethical values such as humanity and humane standards. Western values and the Western community of values have been repeatedly praised in the past. But fundamental values have often been ignored, values which are European values but are also primarily universal values, and whose disregard results in inhumanity:

- nonviolence and respect for life;

- solidarity and a fair economic order;

- truthfulness and tolerance;

- equality and partnership.

Various international conferences and initiatives have stressed the necessity for global ethical standards. The International Commission on Global Governance (1995) emphasized the importance of human rights accompanied by human responsibilities. The World Commission on Culture and Development (1995) demanded, over and above the promotion of economic growth, an investment in human development. Finally, the proposal by the InterAction Council, a conglomeration of former heads of state and government, asked for a Universal Declaration of Human Responsibilities (1997). All of these institutions and their moral appeals were reacting against certain global developments and trends:

- the radically changed international geopolitical reality coupled with the ineffectual proclamation of a "new world order";

- widespread, serious problems with regard to the environment, the population explosion, and energy shortages;

- the increasing trend towards ethnic conflicts and the threat of a clash of cultures at local and regional levels;

- the global interconnectedness which has arisen from developments in communication technologies with their many positive but sometimes also negative considerations;

- the challenges and opportunities of multicultural societies, which nowadays are present not merely in big cities but also in rural areas.

(4) Human responsibilities strengthen human rights

In its first chapter, the Declaration Toward a Global Ethic of the Parliament of the World's Religions (Chicago, 4 September 1993) already affirmed the *fundamental importance of human rights*: "We are convinced of the fundamental unity of the human family on Earth. We recall the 1948 Universal Declaration of Human Rights of the United Nations. What it formally proclaimed on the level of *rights* we wish to confirm and deepen here from the perspective of an *ethic*: The full realization of the intrinsic dignity of the human person, the inalienable freedom and equality in principle of all humans, and the necessary solidarity and interdependence of all humans with each other." But the declaration also emphasizes "that actions in favor of rights and freedoms presume a consciousness of responsibility and duty, and that therefore both the minds and hearts of women and men must be addressed."

In this point, the Declaration Toward a Global Ethic agrees with Article 29 of the Universal Declaration of Human Rights in that it expressly states that "everyone has duties to the community." The article also refers to "the just requirements of morality, public order and the general welfare in a democratic society." These considerations were the inspiration for the formulation of the above-mentioned Declaration of Human Responsibilities proposed by the InterAction Council (cf. Chap. IV, 2). It is thus clear that human rights and human responsibilities towards society in general *do not limit each other but fruitfully complement each other*. Various documents by international commissions have also emphasized this point (cf. Chap. IV, 5).

It is well known that in its recent history the term *duty* has often been misused, both by the state and the church. But this misuse should not prevent us from retaining the term, which has a long history dating back to Cicero and Ambrose. Kant made the term into a key concept of modernity and it remains irreplaceable today.

Duty exerts a moral pressure but it does not force a person to do something. Duty follows not primarily from technical or economic reasons but from ethical reasoning, which recommends and urges a person—who has the faculty of free choice—to act morally. And it should not be forgotten that not only duties but also rights can be misused: when these rights are, firstly, used only to the person's own advantage and, secondly, when these rights are maximally exploited to their fullest capacity. A person who neglects his duties will, in the end, also undermine his rights. Even the state is jeopardized if its citizens, and even more if those who bear ultimate political and economic responsibility, do not make reasonable use of their rights and duties, preferring to misuse them for their own self-interest alone. It is unnecessary to make explicit reference to the pertinent political and economic scandals which have occurred in the Federal Republic of Germany.

Obviously, the legal application of human rights must not depend in any way on the performance of duties. This would imply that rights are only due to those persons who have shown themselves to be worthy of them through the fulfilment of their duties towards society. But this would clearly violate the unconditional *dignity of the human person*, which in turn is a precondition for both rights and duties.

(5) A common basis despite diversity

A global ethic demands that *cultural and religious diversity* must be respected and thus the different legislation and laws in various countries and regions must also be respected, as long as they do not run contradictory to universal human rights. It is, for example, completely understandable that the Jewish State of Israel has made adherence to the Sabbath rest on Saturday a legal requirement. And it is equally understandable that Friday is accorded a special status even in such relatively liberal Arab countries such as Oman. But it should be equally understandable that traditionally Christian countries support keeping the Sunday as a day of no work, and that a broad alliance of churches, unions, associations, and politicians would like to see the right to a work-free Sunday incorporated in the EU's Working Time Directive as a European cultural asset. The same also applies to religious symbols in public such as crosses in traditionally Catholic regions, as long as such crosses are not misused for party-political or church-political ends.

But despite cultural and religious diversity, a global ethic draws particular attention to ethical commonalities. Everyone together bears responsibility for society and humanity. And this poses the challenge of establishing a common moral basis as a basis for decisions and actions: not a complex ethical system but a system which nonetheless consists of a few generally accepted elementary and ethical key norms.

A global ethic is thus a transcultural central idea which can serve as the basis for a pluralistic and often multicultural society. A global ethic assumes, as a matter of course, that the contextual roots of and justifications for ethical principles, values, and standards differ. The justification of a global ethic is by no means limited to religious options. Instead, a global ethic is an appeal— an inclusive appeal—to commit to ethical values and standards: an appeal which is directed at believers and nonbelievers, at religious and nonreligious persons alike. No one is exempt from this appeal, not even those who are making the appeal.

And the relevance of the idea of a global ethic for different areas of society is becoming increasingly evident:

- in *education*: as the mix of pupils in classes becomes increasingly ethnically diverse, while at the same time a basic ethical orientation is increasingly expected; in *politics*: nationally, politics depend on a foundation of shared basic values, particularly in times of deep-seated change, not least because social cohesion must be preserved by a balance of freedoms and responsibilities;

- in the *economy*: in an age of globalization the economy must offer proof of its dependability by its commitment to elementary ethical standards, not merely within a company in the form of a company ethical code (business culture, code of conduct) or in business relations—which are now increasingly intercultural—where economic capital and trust matter, but quite fundamentally in helping to shape our globalized economy;

- in *international relationships*: agreeing to a basic humane ethic can have a lasting impact for peace between people in the different areas of the world.

2. Clearing away misunderstandings

The Global Ethic Project was launched more than two decades ago and included the programmatic statements: No peace among nations without peace between religions. No peace between religions without a dialogue between religions. No dialogue between religions without shared elementary ethical values, standards, and attitudes.

Today, the Global Ethic Project is accepted all over the world in many societies, receives copious comments by the media, and is being implemented at many levels, particularly in schools. Nevertheless, misunderstandings about the Project still abound. I would, therefore, like to start by clearing up a few of these misunderstandings which continually reappear.

(1) The Global Ethic Project is not an explicitly religious project — it is a project based on a general ethic

The Global Ethic Project can and should be supported by religious and nonreligious persons alike. Philosophical justifications are equally possible as are theological arguments, or reasoning based on the study of religions.

(2) A global ethic is not merely an ethic for individuals; it applies at all times to all persons and institutions

The Declaration Toward a Global Ethic proclaimed in 1993 in Chicago expresses "what the fundamental elements of a global ethic for humankind should be—for individuals as well as for communities and organizations, for states as well as for the religions themselves."

(3) The Global Ethic Project does not aim to create a unified and uniform religion but strives for peace between the religions

A unity of the Christian *churches* would be possible if it was not thwarted by the governing bodies of some churches, particularly the Roman-Catholic church because they wish to maintain power. All Christian churches have a shared foundation through their common belief in Jesus Christ. But such a shared foundation of belief is lacking among the large *world religions*, and the aim must be not to strive for a unity of the religions but to strive for dialogue, cooperation, and peace between them.

(4) Peace between the religions means not ignoring the differences between religions but surmounting them

Differences in teachings, rites, and practices must be taken seriously, but at the same time – for the sake of the future of humankind – it is necessary to emphasize the existence of certain shared ethical norms despite existing differences. Whoever takes the idea of a global ethic seriously is often more knowledgeable about the differences between religions than certain Christian apologists who only emphasize the differences without looking at what the religions have in common.

(5) Although religions are often competing against one another, a shared strategy to foster peace is possible

Indian and Chinese religions are not directed so strongly against others as the three prophetic religions. But despite their significant differences in dogma, Judaism, Christianity, and Islam have a lot in common, in particular important ethical standards which form the core of a global ethic. These ethical commonalities would make a constructive cooperation in the service of peace possible between these religions.

Admittedly, each of the three prophetic religions would have to make use of their considerable potential for peace and critically reexamine those areas that have the potential to trigger conflicts. This would apply, for example, to the question of "holy war" in both the Koran and the Hebrew Bible, and to the dogmatic exclusiveness of Christological statements, for instance in the Gospel of St. John. A global ethic on the other hand emphasizes those statements in holy writings which foster peace and unity, without ignoring their potential for conflict.

(6) A global ethic does not mean a new global ideology but represents a realistic vision

Today, modern unifying ideologies, whether socialist, capitalist, scientific, or even religious, are less and less convincing. A global ethic is not an artificial superstructure; it does not represent an "artificially abstract, global, unitary ethic." It respects the diversity of moral cultures based on religion and philosophy and does not make well-meaning attempts to repress the beliefs of dissenters. It is based on the ancient wisdom of cultures and on elementary rules of conduct which have developed since humanity evolved from the animals and which found their expression in the religious and ethical traditions of different cultures as well as common law.

(7) A global ethic does not want to replace the ethic of individual religions—it wants to support it

Religion is more than a set of moral standards; in the first instance, it is a message, a doctrine of salvation. But religion also includes rites and forms the basis for a community. It would be folly and illusion to think of replacing or improving on the Jewish Torah, the Christian Sermon on the Mount, the Muslim Koran, the Hindu Bhagavad-Gita, the teachings of Buddha, or the sayings of Confucius. They remain the foundation and framework for the beliefs, lives, thoughts, and actions of hundreds of millions of people. The religions should, nay must, retain what is distinctive to them and emphasize it in their religious doctrines, rites, and communities. But at the same time, they must also recognize and realize what they have in common with regard to certain elementary ethical directives.

(8) A global ethic does not reduce religions to an ethical minimum but stresses a shared core of elementary human rules of conduct

A global ethic emphasizes the fundamental aspects of what the world religions already have in common in their ethic. The two basic principles of a global ethic are ambitious and significantly improve human coexistence: the Rule of Humanity, i.e., that every person must be treated humanely and not inhumanely or brutally, and the Golden Rule of Reciprocity, i.e., that one should not do to another—neither to an individual nor to a group—that which one would not like to have done to oneself.

(9) A global ethic is not a program of the West which needs to be imposed on the rest of the world; it is nourished by all great world cultures

Basic moral norms have developed in all cultures. The emphasis on humanity and the Golden Rule of Reciprocity can be found in the sayings of Confucius collected five centuries before Christ. The four central ethical directives or imperatives of humanity—do not kill, do not steal, do not lie, do not abuse sexuality—are found in the teachings of Patañjali, the compiler of the Yoga Sutras, in the Buddhist canon, and, of course, in the Hebrew Bible, the New Testament, and the Koran.

(10) A global ethic does not decide on ethical questions which are notoriously contested between or within religions

Those ethical questions about which no consensus between the religions or even within a religion is possible cannot be at this point in time the subject matter of a global ethic. That is why the Declaration Toward a Global Ethic issued by the Parliament of the World's Religions did not include four problems about which there is currently no consensus: contraception, abortion, homosexuality, and euthanasia. But, rather than polarizing society in these disputed matters as so often occurs, the religions have a duty and responsibility to contribute to a consensus which will help individuals and contribute to social peace through further reflection on these questions and through discussions based on general ethical norms.

3. Essential aspects

(1) Ethic does not mean a moral philosophy but a moral consciousness, conviction, and attitude

Strictly speaking, "ethic" (from the Greek, originally meaning custom, tradition, or habit) does not mean "ethics." In other words, it does not stand for an ethical system, a philosophical or theological doctrine, or discipline (e.g., the ethics of Aristotle, of Thomas Aquinas, of Immanuel Kant), all of which are, of course, very important as they are scholarly reflections on moral behavior. Ethic means an inner moral conviction and a comprehensive attitude, a commitment by a person to binding values, unshake-able standards, and personal basic attitudes or virtues. Ethic is not sited at the level of the law, of external rules, of laws and para-graphs, of the police, public prosecutors, courts, or prisons. Ethic is sited at the level of personal conscience—or, to use the term used in other cultural traditions, of the heart—that is, at the level of the inner moral compass. Legal and ethical levels are both necessary, they draw on and support each other, and neither may ignore or absorb the other.

(2) Ethical values, norms, and basic attitudes are culturally specific and rooted in their time, and yet universal ethical constants also exist

Ethical norms are always implemented in a particular situation, in a specific place, at a specific time, and amongst the people living there. They are implemented in very different ways. Because they are rooted in their time and depend on the specific constellation, at different times norms will not only be implemented according to changing priorities, they may even disappear, be forgotten, even—often for reasons of power—consciously ignored. Think, for example, of the disregard of Jesuanic nonviolence in the time of the crusades or the partly culturally sanctioned killing of girls in South and East Asia.

But certain fundamental ethical standards apply (or should apply) in all cultures. Experience has shown that similar life-values emerge again and again, even in very different cultural worlds. They include, first and foremost, the protection of life, of property, of truth (honesty), of sexuality. All cultures have called for similar norms. And yet it is also a truism that basic values such as truthfulness and justice are understood differently in China or India compared to Europe or the United States. And of course, attitudes to sexuality and partnership have changed much over the centuries.

Yet murder, theft, falsehood, and fornication that threaten life, property, truthfulness, and sexuality were and are considered, everywhere and at all times, morally reprehensible, even if in different ways. Irrespective of whether it is an American, an Israeli, a German president, a British prime minister, or a Japanese political leader who is misleading or lying to his people, sooner or later he will be held publicly accountable and punished by the loss of trust and voters' support or even required to resign. And whether he is the CEO of a company in New York, Tokyo, Singapore, or Frankfurt, he will usually face a loss of credibility and can expect legal sanctions, even if he is immune to the pangs of his own conscience. Whether the person who rapes a woman or abuses a child is a prominent politician or a man of the church, the public will accord him no mercy, regardless of whether, in the end, he can be prosecuted in court or not.

(3) A global consensus is only possible and necessary for basic moral concepts

A global consensus is possible for basic moral concepts, moral theories which are limited to certain rudimentary requirements. These are the only basic moral concepts that can be expected of other nations, cultures, and religions and promoted worldwide: the protection of life, of justice, of sexuality, and of truthfulness. They are the necessary requirements of a pure morality that must never be relinquished.

A consensus is not necessary for culturally differentiated morality, which necessarily includes numerous culture-specific elements (certain forms of democracy or education). No levelling demands that the moral assessment and practice be the same should be made of other nations, cultures, or religions for such contested areas as abortion or euthanasia.

(4) Conflicts of norms in specific contexts demand a careful consideration of their respective merits

A global ethic does not mean a purely normative ethic but an ethic of responsibility: an ethic which does not merely take ethical norms into account but also the consequences which can result from the observance of the norm. Norms that take no account of a situation are hollow. Situations without norms are blind. Conflicts of norms and conflicts of duty are not rare in specific situations; in fact, such conflicts are usually the rule.

Things are rarely black or white, right or wrong. The person or persons involved must carefully consider the merits of their actions according to their conscience in a way which does not suspend the norms but which accords preference to the higher good (for example, saving the life of a concealed Jew in Nazi times) above the lesser good (telling the truth to the secret police). In such circumstances, it then becomes both understandable and morally justifiable for a person to risk his own life and that of others to end political tyranny (such as an assassination attempt on Hitler). But even when it is not a matter of the great questions of life and death—a manager's day-to-day decisions, a journalist's reports, balancing opposing interests in daily life—it is usually necessary to weigh and balance competing goods and interests. Standards are necessary; there can be no ethical attitude without standards.

(5) Ethical rules can be developed and lived based on reason alone, without recourse to a transcendent authority

Today, many enlightened individuals who attempt to think and live according to ethical principles dispense with a religious justification of their ethic because they are not religious. Far too often, religion has led to rigorism, obscurantism, superstition, and has misled people, acting as an opiate. Religious people cannot and should not deny that many people have a basic ethical orientation and lead moral lives even without religion. In point of fact, many of those persons in modern times who have championed human dignity and human rights, freedom of conscience, and freedom of religion have more often been nonreligious than religious, and as such have become models for religious people as well.

It must be emphasized that, in principle, insofar as human beings are rational beings, they are endowed with a truly human autonomy, an autonomy which provides them with a basic confidence in reality even without a belief in God which allows them to perceive and perform their responsibilities in the world. This includes their responsibility towards themselves and their responsibility towards the world. Since Aristotle and Stoicism, philosophy has developed and realized goals and priorities, values and norms, ideals and models, and criteria for true and false based on reason. This will be expanded upon further in the next chapter.

(6) It will be difficult to convince people from different cultures and backgrounds using purely rational and abstract arguments

The discourse ethics of *Karl-Otto Apel* (b. 1922) and *Jürgen Habermas* (b. 1929), which focused on justifying normativity rightly emphasized the importance of a rational consensus and discourse. They believed that it would be possible to develop norms, independent of context, which would always be applicable based on communicative and argumentative exchanges between individuals. Religious justifications and interpretations of morality which, they alleged, had lost their value in the eyes of the general public should be replaced by rational discourse, by a procedural language-game, by the "constraint of unconstrained argument." While every religious line of argument also presupposes a rational involvement, in view of the concrete circumstances it is questionable whether an ethic can be propagated globally and spread (until it has spread to the smallest Indian or African village) based on abstract rational discourse alone. Philosophy can demonstrate that certain norms are justified and obligatory. Religion, however, if understood properly, can provide additional motivation, and norms can only claim to be unconditionally valid when mediated through the prism of religion—through reference to an unconditional authority.

(7) An ethical coalition of religious and nonreligious people and groups is a sociopolitical and global political necessity

Rapid scientific, technological, and industrial developments have made global challenges—whether of a political, social, ecological, cultural, or individual nature—so complex and pressing that they can only be managed through the cooperation of different social groups, both religious and nonreligious. A common ethic is essential for this: peaceful coexistence demands a mutual agreement to nonviolently resolve conflicts between nations, ethnicities, and religions. A fair economic and legal order demands the will to abide by a certain order and by specific laws. Institutions at a local, regional, national, or international level can only function with at least tacit assent of the citizens involved.

A civilized coexistence in families, during sports activities, or at work requires a minimum of mutual respect and a willingness to deal fairly and decently with one another. But the disappearance of old traditions and authorities which served as an orientation has led, in many societies, to a profound crisis of orientation and the danger of an existential and normative vacuum bare of moral values. This can lead to egoism and indifference, and often to trivial nihilism and diffuse cynicism. We therefore also need to put traditional antagonisms—conservatives against liberals, those who champion a religious state against those who advocate secularism, propagandists of a premodern Christian Europe against apologists of a purely secular Europe—behind us and transcend them.

Even the quarrel about the true origin of human rights can be put into perspective if two things are considered: the explicit formulation of human rights and human dignity as inviolable and inalienable is indisputably a momentous service which must be laid at the door of European Enlightenment (Aufklärung, Les Lumières) in the 17th/18th century. But it developed in Europe and could only develop in Europe because of its Judeo-Greek-Christian heritage (the human being as an individual, a person, an image of God) from Plato, Aristotle and the Stoics, to Thomas Aquinas, and further to the contributions of Spanish Baroque scholasticism and international law (Vitoria, Las Casas).

(8) Religious traditions must not be ignored but need to be reflected on critically

Cultural anthropology has much to teach us, as we can see by taking a closer look. Specific ethical norms, values, and insights developed gradually as part of highly complex socio-dynamic processes. Guidelines and regulations for human behavior have always suggested themselves wherever necessities of life arose, where interpersonal pressures and needs became apparent: specific conventions, directives, and traditions, in other words, ethical standards, rules, and norms which human beings have tested for millennia were adopted. It is striking how much certain ethical norms resemble each other everywhere in the world. It is also a matter of historical fact that for centuries religions were the systems which provided practical guidelines, which formed the basis for specific moralities and which legitimized, explained, and often sanctioned this morality through punishment. This will be discussed in more detail later.

Originally, when questions of morality were reflected on and guidelines developed, both philosophy and religion and philosophy and theology interacted symbiotically within closed cultural spheres. Such closed spheres cannot be recreated; ethical questions today extend far beyond such a framework of philosophy, religion, and individual cultures. A more intensive cooperation between all relevant disciplines is required with the same vision of hope in mind: "to make the world a better place." The basis for realizing this vision of hope must consist of a shift in attitudes towards a humane ethic—an ethic in the service of a culture of nonviolence and respect for all life, of solidarity and a fair economic order, tolerance, and a life in truthfulness, a culture of equality and partnership between men and women against all forms of inhumanity.

II.

How Can a Global Ethic be Justified?

In practice, many different justifications for a common ethic exist. I differentiate between seven types of justification: pragmatic, philosophical, cultural-anthropological, political, legal, physiological-psychological, and theological. The personal background included here which may interest the reader is, as already mentioned in the introduction, not autobiographical (the third volume of my memoirs will provide detailed information on that) but takes the shape of a history of research: a brief account of the groundwork involved and preceding events. In the following it should become clear that these are no carelessly drafted, ad hoc theses; they are based on knowledge which was long in the gathering, difficult to acquire, and tested in many disputes. I will start with a pragmatic justification for which many examples would serve. My example is sports, an area which has lately been hit by many scandals.

1. Pragmatic justification: Can people live together successfully without moral standards?

Personal background: Initially, these deliberations were prompted by a talk on sports law held by my Rotarian friend Dr. Alfred Sengle, President of the Court and corporate counsel to the German Football Association (DFB). Latterly, sports law, which only a few years ago played a relatively minor role in law, has expanded greatly. Sports law for certain types of sports now fills whole tomes.

My question during the discussion was whether it would only be possible to get to the root of the new problems and scandals by creating even more legal clauses. Dr. Sengle was quite aware of the dangers of increasing juridification and of the necessity of an ethic without which laws cannot properly function. He was able to put me in touch with the German Football Association and the German Protestant Kirchentag, where on May 27, 2005, in Hanover the topic Ethic and Sport was up for debate.

The former President of the German Football Association, Dr. Theo Zwanziger, was keen for the German Football Association to focus not only on sporting successes showcasing the national team but for the association to also show its commitment to moral standards among its rank and file, its associations, and clubs. His main concern was to use the sport and its popularity among the general public as a social and cultural force to promote integration, tolerance, respect, justice, and fair play across all boundaries and across the different ages, beliefs, and states.

And so, on May 27, 2005, I gave the introductory lecture at the Kirchentag on "A Global Sports Ethic" to the forum in a large exhibition hall. My suggestions and ideas were taken up and expanded in subsequent discussions and interviews. All the prominent guests, from the IOC member (and later President of the German Olympic Sport Federation) Dr. Thomas Bach to Per Mertesacker from the German National Football Team, the referee Lutz-Michael Fröhlich to Sylvia Schenk, former President of the German Cycling Federation, the sociologist Gunter A. Pilz, renowned for his research on violence, to the DFB coach Joachim Löw, took a decided stance and offered insights into their personal experiences.

On September 27th of the same year, I participated in a panel debate held in the Paulskirche in Frankfurt which was hosted by the International Olympic Forum. The discussion followed a talk given by the President of the International Olympic Committee (IOC), Dr. Jacques Rogge. I was able to highlight the clear parallels between the Olympic Charter and the ethical code of the IOC Ethics Commission on the one side and the Declaration Toward a Global Ethic on the other: the Olympic ethic is an intercultural ethic. The discussion went so well that I subsequently invited Jacques Rogge to give the Global Ethic Lecture at Tübingen University. On May 10, 2006, he gave a talk in the university's Great Hall on the topic "Global Sport and Global Ethic." For my part, I have since systematically reconsidered the problems and formulated a pragmatic justification of a global ethic.

(1) Every game—from chess to football—needs rules

Football cannot be played without rules. It is the rules of the game that create the freedom within which the game can develop. Football demonstrates, as do other team sports, that a good, fair, and interesting game can only be achieved by sticking to the rules. Rules do not constitute a burden—they are liberating!

(2) Fair play—a game played according to the rules— requires that ethical norms are observed

Referees, usually models of fairness, have latterly brought general disrepute to a previously unimpeachably honest profession through corruption and the manipulation of match results. The pharmaceutical manipulations of racing cyclists and their medical, sports, and psychological supervisors have ensured that not only individual racing cyclists appear as cheaters and liars—they have discredited professional cycling as a whole, making it appear an unsportsmanlike, unfair, and immoral sport. This is more than merely violating sports law, a law which has become ever more detailed and complicated over the past few decades; it is a violation of elementary basic values of human decency: truthfulness, justice, solidarity, and humanity. The issue is the betrayal of an idea, the spirit of sports, which is increasingly being sacrificed to commercial interests.

True fair play means more than just the observance of rules specific to the sport enforced by the threat of sanctions. Fair play stands for "a general mental attitude emanating from the duty to adhere to ethical principles, with these rules also being affirmed internally; where, although athletes strive their utmost to be successful, success will nevertheless not be achieved at all costs; where an opponent is not an enemy who must be defeated using any means possible but is respected as a partner in a sports competition who must be accorded the right of equal opportunity and whose physical integrity and human dignity must be respected regardless of his nationality, race or origin." ("Karlsruhe Declaration on Fair Play" of the German Association for Sports Law, 1998).

(3) Global sports need a global ethic

Each sport has its own rules but it doesn't require a special and separate ethic. It only needs to adhere to the general basic principles which apply to all areas of life—politics, the economy, culture, public, and private life. In the secularized, individualistic, and pluralistic world of today, these ethical rules, which have gradually prevailed and which were formulated and promoted by different religious and philosophical traditions, are often no longer self-evident. We need to once again be made aware of them, starting with the family, in kindergartens, and schools.

An era which has seen the unprecedented globalization of sports so that it has permeated to even the smallest nations on our planet needs *global rules*, rules like those which are already taken for granted in football, the most widely known and popular of grassroots sports. Without such rules it would be impossible to have a UEFA Cup or a Champions League—there would be no World Cup and no Olympic Games. But these global rules of play only function if they are supported and underpinned by universal ethical rules of humanity. Otherwise, athletes and officials will repeatedly try to circumvent, ignore, or undermine the written rules of the sport. Thus, worldwide sports need a worldwide ethic: global sports need a global ethic.

(4) The four imperatives of humanity also apply to sports
In my lecture on "A Global Sport Ethic" I described these four imperatives as follows:

"Firstly: All of us who love sports have been appalled, time and again, by the magnitude of the *violence* which sports can unleash and which it attracts. On the playing field, opponents become enemies who must be fought using all conceivable means. The use of violence often violates the physical integrity of the opposing player. Major sports events attract violent groups. The extent of verbal and physical aggression shows the depths to which people can sink. Opponents are provoked and slandered. Fans resort to violence against each other or even against players. Xenophobic aggressions run riot.

It is, therefore, necessary to recall the ancient and universal imperative of humanity to mind, postulated by all religions: *Do not kill*, injure, torment, or torture. Or, to put it in positive terms: Have respect for life! Football and sports in general depend on adherence to this rule and need to contribute to a culture of nonviolence and respect for life.

Secondly: All of us who love sports know what it means when a game, contest, or race is won through corruption, through deliberate deceit, through a wrong decision by the referee or a biased jury, or through some form of injustice.

This is where the ancient, universal imperative of humanity postulated by all religions must come into play: *Do not steal*, cheat, bribe, or corrupt. Or, to put it in positive terms: Act honestly and fairly! Football and sports, in general, depend on adherence to this rule and need to contribute to a culture of solidarity and a just world order.

Thirdly: All of us who love sports know immediately what is meant when we hear the words: he/she has robbed someone of their victory—for example, through doping, through advantages unfairly obtained, through denying their opponent their equal opportunity, through injuring their opponent in a game, through some form of dishonesty.

What is important here is the ancient, universal imperative of humanity postulated by all religions: *Do not lie*, deceive, falsify, or manipulate. Or, to put it in positive terms: Speak and act honestly! Football and sports in general depend on adherence to this rule and should contribute to a culture of truthfulness in which everyone has a right to verity and truthfulness.

Fourthly: It has taken a long time for true *gender equality* to prevail in sports. This has been achieved more in some sports than others. Women have had to struggle to obtain the same opportunities. Women have attracted scorn and disdain in some sports. Unfortunately, their sports performance has often not been taken seriously.

Here the universal imperative now postulated by all religions today must become universally respected: *not to despise the other sex*, not to abuse it, degrade it, and humiliate it; or in positive terms, respect and love each another! Football and sports in general must contribute to a culture of equal opportunities and partnership between men and women.

2. Philosophical justification: To what extent does reason militate in favor of a global ethic?

Personal background: It has always been my conviction that not only religion but also philosophy can and should justify a common basic human ethic. Before studying theology I studied philosophy for six semesters in Rome with passionate interest and wrote my philosophical master's thesis on Jean-Paul Sartre's Existentialism as Humanism (1951). After completing my theological doctorate I focused on Hegel's philosophy (cf. "The Incarnation of God" 1970). Since then I have repeatedly studied the important modern philosophers. In a chapter on "fundamental trust as the basis of ethics "in my philosophical book entitled "Does God Exist? An Answer for Today" published in 1978, I discussed in detail how nonreligious people also shape their lives in accordance with ethical values. All of these ideas together with many others flowed into the book "Projekt Weltethos"(1990) ("Global Responsibility" 1991).

I am grateful for the insights of my colleague Hans-Martin Schönherr-Mann, professor of political philosophy at the University of Munich. In his book "Miteinander leben lernen. Die Philosophie und der Kampf der Kulturen" [Learning to Live with Each Other. Philosophy and the Clash of Civilizations] (Munich 2008) which drew on his outstanding knowledge of the latest analyses of the history of philosophy, he discussed the philosophical presuppositions for a global ethic, citing the most important philosophers of the 20th century. In a subsequent volume—"Globale Normen und individuelles Handeln" [Global Norms and Individual Actions] (Würzburg 2010)—Professor Schönherr-Mann examined various philosophical approaches to a global ethic and developed "the idea of a global ethic from an emancipatory perspective." I will be mainly focusing on some of the arguments of his two books in my discussion below.

(1) Preconditions for the Global Ethic Project in 20th-century philosophy

If we agree with the pragmatism of *William James* and *John Dewey*, then we could take the stance that in view of the plurality of philosophies, we should avoid insoluble problems and not attempt to overcome rivaling worldviews and ideologies, nor should we aim for a unity of religions. Instead, an attempt should be made—regardless of all ideological differences—to moderate the differences between worldviews through the pragmatic resolution of urgent problems. In the longer term, this would lead to certain ethical standards being held in common. This might bring an end to the wars between worldviews or ideologies.

But this pragmatic stance does not sufficiently emphasize the increasing responsibility of humanity. It was therefore clear from the outset that the Global Ethic Project would have to be more along the lines of *Max Weber's* ethics of responsibility as this did not exclude the question of the right worldview but preferred to focus on the consequences for which humanity as an agent must be held answerable. It should be noted that quite early on, *Jean-Paul Sartre* viewed all of human life as the purview of human responsibility. Spurred on by the enormity of the new possibilities generated by modern technology, *Hans Jonas* expanded the responsibilities of humanity to cover the entire biosphere, demanding that the dangerous consequences of technological actions for future generations also need to be considered: humanity bears responsibility for the environment and for later generations.

Jonas' *Imperative of Responsibility* and Ernst Bloch's *Principle of Hope*, which pointed the way to an ecological and global way of thinking, complement each other. In their definition of responsibility, the focus is on interpersonal situations: the difference and foreignness of the other person must be considered and consideration must also be shown to enemies; this idea was expanded by *Emmanuel Lévinas*. It was *Hannah Arendt*, who in her search for a form of responsible communication focused on the need for an "enlarged mentality," on the idea for imagination and a sense of community. She attached particular importance to the virtue of truthfulness because honesty endeavors to elicit factual truths without which open communication between individuals is impossible.

Infinite communication is the precondition for a global ethic discourse. *Karl Jaspers* emphasized the universality of rationality and included philosophy and religion in his search for global and intercultural communication. And the credit for the methodical rethinking of the dialogic concept of understanding, which is the precondition for a common human ethic, must finally go to *Hans-Georg Gadamer*. Admittedly Gadamer and his disciples moved in a world of concepts; it was necessary to make this world of ideas tangible.

(2) How do we achieve a consensus?

The Global Ethic Project is open to the rational justification of ethics, like the justification of *Karl-Otto Apel* (analytical philosophy) and of *Jürgen Habermas* (Critical Theory of the Frankfurt School). Habermas attempted to develop norms based on communication and a deliberative discourse between individuals—norms which must universally apply in a modern democracy—rationality as a principle for nonviolent communication. A conciliatory social consensus can be achieved through processes of argumentation in a noncoercive, unrestricted, deliberative discourse. However, there is always a risk that the modernization of society will be derailed, that the democratic cohesive forces will be weakened, and assumed solidarity eroded. Religion— originally of no social relevance for the Frankfurt School—thus becomes increasingly important for Habermas as it helps us gain an understanding of ourselves with regard to the conditions which make our life humane, tolerable, and not bleak.

It was the American *John Rawls* (1921–2002), who in his political philosophy of the 1970s and 1980s developed a philosophical concept which largely corresponds to that of Global Responsibility (1990/1991) and yet differs from it (cf. J. Rawls, *A Theory of Justice*, Cambridge/Mass. 1971).

It might appear that both concepts are pursuing comparable goals despite their different paths and that both concepts are complementary. Rawls also attempts to construct an overarching philosophical consensus on the principles of fairness required for coexistence. But in all modesty, I opine that on several important points a global ethic is superior to Rawls' *Theory of Justice*:

- Rawls' concept of political justice, understood as fairness, remains bound to the concept of legislative justice, from which he deduces the existence of ethical rules. A global ethic, however, includes the ethical dimension from the outset.

- Rawls deliberately considered concrete contexts and situations in the abstract, within a general and institutional framework. A global ethic is geared towards the concrete and individual.

41

- Rawls' theory is programmatically secularist, and, in contrast to Habermas, he wishes to exclude religious arguments from the political debate. While the arguments of a global ethic are secular, the global ethic remains open to religions without taking sides for or against a religious or nonreligious worldview.

- Rawls' theory of justice is limited by its national perspective; he only attempted, not entirely convincingly, to expand his theory to include the principles and norms of international law and international relationships two decades later (cf. J. Rawls, *The Law of Peoples*, New York, 1999). A global ethic had a global perspective, right from the outset.

The Global Ethic Project is concerned with uncovering a minimum of basic, fundamental ideas on good and evil common to many different worldviews. It looks for concrete, shared, ethical precepts which govern the actions of individuals and the functioning of institutions. A global ethic does not mean a complete ethical consensus and certainly not a single world religion, world culture, or world ideology, but only a basic consensus. What is at issue is a core ethic consisting of a few elementary moral values, standards, and attitudes which can be found in all the great religious and philosophical traditions despite their obvious differences.

(3) Pragmatic acceptance

It would, of course, be possible to examine the different philosophical ethics with regard to their underlying norms. Maybe they will be found to be more or less congruent with those of a global ethic. But in view of the dissensions between philosophers and given the abstractness of their ethical treatises which are barely understood by the world at large, Hans-Martin Schönherr-Mann pragmatically recommends accepting the empirical findings from the history of religions: "In view of the fact that a concept for a global ethic already exists and that it is one which was approved of by the representatives of the world's religions at the 1993 conference in Chicago, the philosophical task is to examine whether it is possible to assent to those ethical guidelines promoted at the 1993 conference. The core of the *Declaration Toward a Global Ethic* consists of the following four principles: nonviolence and respect for life as enshrined in the commandment not to kill; solidarity and a fair economic order as enshrined in the commandment not to steal; tolerance and truthfulness as enshrined in the commandment not to lie; equal rights and partnership between men and women as enshrined in the commandment not to commit fornication."

Philosophers today often do not want to or cannot supply an ultimate philosophical justification of fundamental ethical norms. It is conceivable that initially—not least in view of the current global situation—we could start with a global consensus on fundamental global ethical norms. This does not preclude philosophical reasoning from attempting a (in actual fact penultimate) justification of these fundamental human norms and their consensus. That would be an important contribution towards a global ethic.

Religious and philosophical justifications can complement each other; philosophy can critically review religious norms, rendering them more precise, correcting them, and making them more concrete. The modern philosophy of language, for example, has pointed out that truthfulness, trust, and dependability are preconditions for human communication (including for toddlers just learning to speak). But other vitally important rules, standards, and norms for peaceful human coexistence have also developed, as cultural anthropology has demonstrated.

3. Cultural anthropological justification: Since when has a global ethic existed?

Personal background: If you want to understand the present, you need to know your history, including prehistory when possible. I have always been extremely interested in the origins of humanity since I first studied Sigmund Freud's criticism of religion (cf. "Does God Exist" 1980, Chapt. C III). I prefaced my trilogy of the three Abrahamic religions in my volume on Judaism (1992) with a "brief reflection on global history." According to astrophysical research, the world has existed for more than 13 billion years. Human beings have existed on our planet for perhaps 1,500,000 years. Homo sapiens, as modern persons are proud to call themselves, have existed for perhaps 200,000 years, since the Paleolithic era. The native inhabitants or indigenous peoples of the American continent and of Australia, Polynesia, and Melanesia still attest to this Stone Age period. I met many in the course of my earlier travels.

I was only able to engage with the question of indigenous inhabitants in more detail in connection with trips made to New Guinea, northern Australia, and Africa. The important insight for me was that even in the remote highlands of New Guinea no society, village community, or kinship groups existed without a specific body of norms, laws, and rules regulating human coexistence. A tribesman in New Guinea walking by himself on a country road wearing only a loincloth and carrying a stone ax reminded me that even in these archaic societies not only the respect for life but also the protection of property and, finally, also the respect for—and protection of—sexual relationships is fundamentally important.

It was this insight that later led me to talk of the existence of a primordial ethic—but not of a primordial religion. The debate about the existence of a primordial religion, an issue fervently discussed in the 19th century, ended in a standoff between the proponents of a theory of degeneration who posited a gradual decline from humankind's adherence to monotheistic beliefs and their opponents who supported the concept of humankind's evolutionary development and gradual advance, starting from basic animistic beliefs. Today, researchers are agreed that these phenomena and phases interpenetrate each other. No primordial religion has been found, and religion appears everywhere in different forms. The development of religion is too varied and complex. It increasingly became clear to me that quite a different story applies to a primordial ethic. A brief systematic synopsis must suffice here (cf. "The Beginning of All Things" 2005, Chapter E).

(1) Human beings evolved from the animals but hold an exceptional position among them

Developmentally, human beings have a lot in common with their nearest relatives, the apes: the similarities range from the number of chromosomes, the position of the teeth, and the development of the brain to social behavior and certain early stages of awareness of the self.

Nevertheless, the exceptional position of Homo sapiens among the animals, of human beings as they exist today, cannot be denied. From the start, a characteristic feature of human beings was their upright walk (holding the body upright)—today

45

sometimes taken as a symbol for the ethical deportment of humanity. Homo sapiens is characterized by a consciousness of the self, which has also become an ethical concept—the precondition for a complex syntactic language specific to human beings alone. Humanity's capacity for strategic thinking, abstract thought, and self-reflection is based on language. But inherent to humanity are also directional emotions such as love and hate, hopes and fears, beliefs and wishes. All of these created a foundation for the higher cultural development of humanity and, in particular, for a human ethic.

(2) Evolution has made human beings both spiritual and instinct-driven

Humanity has a double nature: a spirituality, which also always encompasses physicality. A spiritual arrogance of humanity over animals is therefore as misplaced as any biologistic leveling or equating humankind with animals.

The development of humankind was a highly complex process.

Evolutionary biologists tell us that human beings were initially genetically programmed to be *egoistical* and in the early stages of evolution they had to be, to ensure their own survival. But to state that genes are egoistical and that new species only develop by chance is to consider only one side of evolution. The other is that new species and organisms do not develop through selection alone but also through cooperation, creativity, and communication and this is the only way in which evolution can continue to become ever more differentiated.

Amongst the higher animals it is already possible to discern genetically inherent cooperative behavior, particularly among related animals with similar genes: in other words, a kind of *mutual altruism*. Tit for tat: something is given in the expectation of receiving something back. Thus, rudimentary ethical behavior is already rooted in humanity's biological nature; his capacity for morality is, so to speak, innate. Today, many scientific disciplines are looking into these questions and it is becoming ever more apparent that humanity's nature is also primarily designed for empathy and cooperation and not alone for a simple, egoistical survival of the fittest. A mechanistically biological interpretation alone does not suffice to explain the origins of humanity's ethical values and standards.

(3) Human beings had to learn to behave humanely

Sociologists have emphasized the sociocultural factors which are important for ethical development. Only human beings combine the faculty of speech with a unique capacity for cooperation, and this capacity had to be learned in and through social interaction. As strategic thinking evolved, the capacity for *empathy* developed: the capacity to sympathize with others and empathize with their fears, expectations, and hopes, even—particularly within the bounds of a kinship group—a capacity for altruism. This became fundamentally important for human social behavior. And so, over time, moral emotions and intuitions developed which preceded moral arguments and judgments.

Thus, from primeval times, human beings gradually learned to behave *humanely*. Human beings are the only living creatures that have shown themselves to be capable of setting up social and cultural norms early on and have continued to develop them. Already during the dawn of humankind, wherever fundamental needs appeared, wherever interpersonal pressures and necessities became apparent, guidelines for behavior emerged: specific conventions and traditions—in other words, ethical standards, rules, norms, and directives. These guidelines have been tested everywhere in the human race over the course of thousands of years. As one generation succeeded the next, these guidelines became ingrained.

(4) Even indigenous people have a basic ethic which helps to make life and survival possible, and which has remained fundamentally important for the coexistence of human beings up until the present day: a primeval ethic

It is true that indigenous people developed neither writing, science, nor complex technologies. But their thinking is logical, plausible, and marked by a passion to order such things as human relationships. In early tribal cultures (and in those which still exist today) such values and standards took the form of unwritten norms, not tenets. These norms constituted the ethos of the family, the clan, or the tribe and were passed on in the form of stories, parables, allegories, or traditions.

But it was not a coincidence that very similar norms developed in very different regions all over the globe. The norms focused on four vital social areas.

- In the first instance, a respect for life: prohibiting the killing of humans as one would kill animals, with certain exceptions (to settle conflicts or punish violence).

- Regulations to protect the relationships between the sexes: up until the present day, the rules governing who can be allowed to marry whom remain highly complex among Australian aborigines and are far more complicated than in modern societies.

- Regulations to protect property: the Neolithic revolution meant that, in addition to nomadic hunter-gatherers and fishermen, increasing numbers of people began to settle down, cultivate land, and domesticate animals. This led to a desire to own land and private property.

- Regulations to protect the truth: particularly in sophisticated civilizations and religions, truthfulness and reliability became increasingly important, as did being respected and esteemed (honored) by other people for particular human qualities. This understanding of truth is particularly in evidence in the Hebrew Bible: "emet" means "fidelity, constancy, dependability."

These four aspects are fundamental for a proper understanding of the concept of a global ethic: ethical principles and values do not have to be imposed or artificially foisted upon humanity. They correspond to an ethical stance inherent to humankind based on humanity's essential nature and development, and humanity's need to be made aware of them again for human coexistence to succeed.

Latterly, even in ethnology which, quite understandably, originally focused more on cultural differences, emphasis is now being directed towards *cultural similarities* common to all people: similarities in facial expressions (positive smile, frowning), gestures (hands moving up and down in a gesture of moderation), social behavior (forming cliques, gossip), hierarchies (seating important people in a raised position). Researchers have begun investigating questions such as: why has no culture propagated the public performance of the sexual act? Why does everyone have a sense of home? (cf. Christoph Antweiler, Heimat Mensch. *Was uns alle verbindet*, Hamburg 2009) A systematic ethnological investigation into the similarities between human cultures in protecting life, sexual relationships, property, and truth would be very enlightening.

4. Political justification: What should be the basic values of modern society?

Personal background: As a Swiss national, since my youth, I have been deeply interested in national and international politics. I have always tried to investigate matters in detail before permitting myself to publish political analyses and judgments. I have never considered myself a politician, a political scientist, or a political theologian, but since publishing "On Being a Christian," I've been considered a socially critical theologian and philosopher. Invitations to give lectures and hold conferences, among other places in the UN headquarters in New York, at the UNESCO in Paris, and at the World Economic Forum in Davos prompted me to consider global political questions in more detail. Without this focus and without countless conversations with colleagues from many different fields, working in Tübingen or at other universities and in other committees, the volumes "Global Responsibility" (1990/1991) and *A Global Ethic for Global Politics and Economics* (1997)—my most overtly political books, political in the widest sense of the word—would have been impossible. The book "Friedenspolitik. Ethische Grundlagen internationaler Beziehungen" (2003) [Peace Policies. The Ethical Foundations of International Relationships], edited together with the peace and conflict researcher Dieter Senghaas, developed out of the symposium "A new paradigm of international relationships," a symposium of political scientists and philosophers held in Tübingen in the shadow of the wars in Afghanistan and Iraq.

Thus, right from the outset, the Global Ethic Project had a political dimension. The importance of a global ethic for global politics was subsequently discussed by various speakers invited by the Global Ethic Foundation after 2000 to deliver the Global Ethic Lectures at Tübingen University: Prime Minister Tony Blair, UN High Commissioner for Human Rights Mary Robinson, UN Secretary-General Kofi Annan, President of the Federal Republic of Germany Horst Köhler, Nobel Peace Prize Laureate Shirin Ebadi, IOC President Jacques Rogge, former Chancellor of the Federal Republic of Germany Helmut Schmidt, Archbishop Desmond Tutu, Group Chairman of HSBC Holdings Stephen Green, and Prime Minister of Baden-Württemberg Winfried Kretschmann, among others.

(1) In modern society, Christian values can only be meaningfully and effectively advocated within the context of universal human values

In today's pluralistic world, it is neither realistic nor legitimate to stipulate that all men and women living in the Federal Republic of Germany or even in Europe must—for reasons of state and with reference to a unified Europe—adhere to Christian values, as Roman-Catholics or fundamentalist Protestants have repeatedly attempted to do. Christian theologians and church leaders must take the standpoints of other religions seriously, including the standpoints of different political and ideological groups, even those of agnostics or nonreligious citizens. Christian values must be perceived and lived against the background and in the context of universal human values.

(2) On the other hand, basic modern democratic values require an ethical foundation for their implementation

It is not enough to wish to commit all people only to the basic modern values of democracy, tolerance, the rule of law, and human rights. This was the approach propagated by French and Belgian secularists, who, while accepting the ideals of classical antiquity and the Enlightenment, refused to acknowledge the contribution of one and a half thousand years of Christianity to Europe's heritage. The widely accepted dictum of the former judge of the German Constitutional Court Ernst-Wolfgang Böckenförde still applies: "The liberal secularized state lives on assumptions which it cannot guarantee itself. That is the great risk it has been prepared to take for the sake of liberty." ("Staat, Gesellschaft, Freiheit" [State, Society, Freedom] 1976) If they are to be implemented, the values of modernity, in particular, democracy, tolerance, the rule of law, and human rights *do not need a common religion for their foundation, but they certainly need a common ethic*—Böckenförde later referred to a "unifying ethic," "a sort of community spirit": an ethic, in other words, which can and should be sustained and supported both by believers from different religions and nonreligious persons.

(3) Modern society can only be held together by a unifying and mandatory global ethic

We are looking at a common historical learning process. We are living in a period of accelerated secularization, of radicalized individualization, and of increasing ideological pluralism. These changes should not be judged purely negatively; it is an ambivalent development with many inherent risks and dangers but also many opportunities and advantages. Human beings must act *freely* but also responsibly, and at the same time, they must confront their individual destiny. In this dynamic and conflicting situation, the human need for security, for spiritual perspectives, for standards of value, for points of reference and orientation which will provide support has increased rather than decreased.

Given these circumstances, what can hold modern society together? The bedrock of modern society cannot be religious fundamentalism, nor can it be arbitrary pluralism; modern society can only be held together by a mandatory and unifying ethic: a basic civic consensus on universal values, standards, and attitudes which combines autonomous self-fulfillment with responsibility and solidarity.

For believers, such an ethic is rooted in a belief in God as the first and ultimate reality and supreme authority. But this ethic can also be shared and supported by nonbelievers based on humane reasons. Thus it can include very different social groups, political parties, nations, and religions. However, the ethical norms and standards, particularly if they are also advocated for by religions or churches, should not act as shackles or chains. They must not exclude or offer moral judgment but invite, prompt, and appeal to a sense of duty: not an authoritarian but a tolerant ethic.

(4) The necessary new social consensus will not be possible without the political will and ethical impulse of those in positions of responsibility

Despite, and partly also because of the extent of globalization, we are living in a time riven by religious and political dissensions, a time rich in bellicose conflicts and yet without orientation. Despite many positive developments, the fact cannot be ignored: we live in a time in which many moral authorities have lost credibility; a time in which many national, cultural, and regrettably also religious institutions have been sucked into the maelstrom of a profound identity crisis. This is a time in which many standards and norms have shifted so that many people, particularly younger people, often no longer know what is good or evil, right or wrong.

Who could, therefore, deny the fact that a new social consensus is necessary, and at a global level? Globalization requires a global ethic. But this will require political will, particularly on the part of those in positions of responsibility. And when difficult steps must be undertaken for a common good, this is almost impossible to do without an ethical impulse: in other words, without a personal sense of responsibility, without a moral momentum, a moral energy. Examples of such moral undertakings include the Marshall Plan, the formulation of the Universal Declaration of Human Rights, and the creation of the foundations of a peacefully united Europe.

The Global Ethic Project is, of course—I cannot emphasize this enough—a decades-long process working toward a shift in attitudes similar to the shifts in attitude which occurred with regard to women's emancipation, ecology, and disarmament. In the process of their realization, the universal normative rules of a global ethic and a global law are constantly being stress-tested in practice.

5. Legal justification: To what extent does a global law presume a global ethic?

Personal background: For me, right from outset, the Global Ethic Project had a constructive and differentiated relationship to the law. I made sure that this was already clearly stated in the seminal first chapter of the Declaration Toward a Global Ethic, issued in Chicago in 1993, entitled "No new global order without a new global ethic."

Since then I have continued to expand this insight. A particular challenge was the invitation extended to me by the Association of Judges of the German Constitutional Court in Karlsruhe to give a lecture on "Global Law and a Global Ethic" on October 28, 2008. The feedback I received after this lecture was so encouraging and so positive that I was invited to give a talk on the same topic in front of the Juristische Studiengesellschaft [Legal Academic Association] at the German Federal Supreme Court on April 20, 2010. The research and discussions undertaken and held in this context prompted me to suggest that the Global Ethic Foundation should hold an international symposium on "Global Ethic, Law and Policy." The symposium was held on November 3 / 4, 2011 at Georgetown University in Washington, D.C.

(1) Without morality, the law cannot survive

What is the relationship between the law and ethics, between a global law and a global ethic? In my use of the term, "global law" covers the existing international body of laws and includes legislation passed by global institutions. The necessity for but also the limitations of the law with regard to ethics are clear: The "Declaration Toward a Global Ethic" of the 1993 Parliament of the World's Religions clearly and programmatically states:

"We are convinced of the fundamental unity of the human family on Earth. We recall the 1948 Universal Declaration of Human Rights of the United Nations. What it formally proclaimed on the level of *rights* we wish to

55

confirm and deepen here from the perspective of an *ethic*: The full realization of the intrinsic dignity of the human person, the inalienable freedom and equality in principle of all humans and the necessary solidarity and interdependence of all humans with each other.

On the basis of personal experiences and the burdensome history of our planet we have learned:

- that a better global order cannot be created or enforced by laws, prescriptions, and conventions alone;

- that the realization of peace, justice, and the protection of Earth depends on the insight and readiness of men and women to act justly;

- that action in favor of rights and freedoms presumes a consciousness of responsibility and duty, and that therefore both the minds and hearts of women and men must be addressed;

- that rights without morality cannot long endure, and that there will be no better global order without a global ethic."

(2) A global ethic is not a form of legal or ethical casuistry but it does provide principles and guidelines for case-based reasoning

As intimated above: universal norms must always be applied so that they take account of the specific situation. Norms that take no account of a situation are hollow. Situations without norms are blind. This means that norms must throw light on a situation and the situation must illustrate the norms. What is morally good is therefore not simply what is good or right in the abstract, but what is good or right in the specific situation: what is appropriate. In other words, an obligation only becomes concrete in a specific situation. But in a specific situation—only the person affected is able to judge in which situation—an obligation can become absolute. This means what we should do always depends on the situation, but in a specific situation what we should do can become categorical: without any ifs or buts. Thus, every concrete moral decision must combine the general normative constant with the particular variables specific to the situation.

A judge must decide a case practically and bindingly—he cannot and must not cling to the abstract norm. Similarly, a global ethic does not make the assessment of individual cases any easier at the outset. Cases can be highly diverse:

- There are innumerable relatively simple cases where positive law is entirely sufficient to make a judgment and where it is not necessary to appeal to universal legal principles or to the principles of a global ethic. There are instances of positive law—such as the obligation to drive on the right side of the road—laid down in the highway code which are in themselves not ethical principles (an obligation to drive on the left of the road would be equally possible), but which can become ethical obligations (driving on the proper side of the road makes the behavior and expectations of others predictable). And thus, even a posited law such as the obligation to drive on the right side of the road can become an ethical duty when it is a matter of life and death.

- But there are also highly complex cases, for example, the trading of derivatives on the stock exchange— financial bets without any trading of real goods. To what extent such trading is immoral must be investigated in detail by financial specialists and specialists in commercial law and commercial ethics. Perhaps DIN standards (The DIN organization develops norms and standards as a service to industry, to the state and to society as a whole.) could also be useful for financial products. But when such trading becomes fraud and theft, then such practices are immoral. Such a derivatives market would have to be forbidden and those contravening the interdiction would have to be punished.

(3) Universal legal principles are underpinned by the principles of a global ethic

It will only be briefly intimated here how the most important universal legal principles are underpinned by ethical principles, as defined in the Declaration Toward a Global Ethic of Chicago.

Two examples are given below:
a. The legal principle of *equity* ("aequitas" in Roman and canonical law): This principle serves as a corrective to the positive norm in borderline cases. It demands that a case be judged according to a natural sense of justice and can substantially contribute to overcoming the discrepancy between actual jurisdiction and the sense of what is truly just. It allows positive law to be administered more flexibly; for example, in criminal law where a penal sentence can be reduced (e.g. when sentencing adolescents) or a penalty increased (within the scope of the penal code). This principle can be understood as the legal application and concrete

manifestation of the first fundamental basis of a humane ethic, namely the Principle of Humanity: Every human being must be treated humanely and not inhumanely!

Of course, the Principle of Humanity must be qualified and elucidated depending on the specific context and situation. What exactly does "humane treatment" mean? From a basic ethical standpoint, it means no human being should be treated inhumanely or "bestially" (cue: concentration camps, gulag, Abu Ghraib!) but should be treated rationally, i.e., humanely, as befits a human being, that is, in accordance with human dignity and the fundamental value assigned to human dignity.

Bestial behavior, of course, can occur also in interpersonal relationships, for example in sexual relationships.

In legal practice this usually sets negative boundaries: it is easier to define what is "inhumane" in practice than what is "humane." In view of the sexual abuse of children and adolescents, the murder of parents, teachers, and schoolmates by juveniles, and the rape of women it is superfluous to address this point further. Ongoing discussions, particularly in the field of labor law, have yet to arrive at a final conclusion and show that it is not always easy to positively define what constitutes humane treatment in the workplace.

b. The legal principle of *good faith* (bona fides): This principle means that the behavior demanded of every human being is the behavior of the sort exhibited by honest and truthfully minded persons. This legal principle is supported by the second fundamental principle of a global ethic, namely the Principle of Reciprocity, the Golden Rule: *Do unto others as you would have others do unto you!*

This Golden Rule of Reciprocity is not a quixotic tenet but an ethical guideline that should be observed and is mostly adhered to, even in the harshly competitive world of trade and in battles between political interests. Thus, competitors and political opponents must also be treated as fellow human beings and not "liquidated" (physically, in the media, or by other means). Even in commerce and politics ethical criteria never lose their validity: lies and deception are neither permitted in companies, nor in banking, nor in foreign policy. But this does not exclude the inevitable compromises and pragmatic solutions of real life.

(4) The principles of a global ethic can provide support for or even be a source of universal principles of international law

This viewpoint is supported by the three characteristics of these ethical principles:

a. These ethical principles are acknowledged and supported by a broad *international consensus*. This consensus is more apparent among religious groups than between nation-states, but most of these groups are themselves transnational and transcultural. Historically these principles have long been recognized and approved—as principles that support the status of custom in common law. As the above-mentioned Global Ethic Lectures in Tübingen have made abundantly clear, the principles of a global ethic are also supported by prominent politicians.

b. Although the principles of a global ethic are not conceived as legal rights and responsibilities (duties), they nevertheless have the *force of an obligation*. They are compulsory standards of behavior which cannot be freely chosen. For example, the condemnation of corruption in business, as described in the declaration, may over time find its expression in an international convention (or common law) against bribery. Legally nonbinding ethical norms have increasingly led to codifications of specific phrases in binding agreements. This has particularly occurred in human rights legislation and international environmental legislation.

c. Some of the principles of the Global Ethic Declaration could serve as *precursors for international legal norms*: they address current problems that have arisen through globalization. The second directive in the declaration, for example, refers to a fair and just economic order. This is relevant for the transnational activities of certain multinational companies which only push for the implementation of rules and regulations that maximize their profits. So how can an ethic be incorporated in law if there is no ethical consensus? Where such an ethical consensus exists, ways of dealing honestly with one another develop very quickly and infringements can easily be made actionable based on a general acceptance of ethical principles.

One example of this is the *lex mercatoria*, a body of law that developed in the late Medieval period "from the bottom up" among the merchants in the Hanseatic cities and which was based on accepted moral conventions. No edicts were necessary for its acceptance, nor were any sanctions necessary "from above" to ensure compliance. Today we can find similar processes occurring with the UN Global Compact. Once again, private individuals and the stakeholders of a civic society have framed an agreement regarding a basic economic ethic and are enforcing this agreement through gentle moral persuasion even in places that cannot be reached by the arm of the law.

It is worth considering the words of the Swiss professor of constitutional law Max Huber, one-time President of the Permanent

Court of International Justice in The Hague and subsequently for many years President of the International Committee of the Red Cross. In 1955/56 Max Huber already developed the term "international ethic" to describe a concept behind and above the law: "The law can be bent like iron if it is not an ethic. But an ethic is like a crystal." Thus several instances in which the second Bush administration bent and twisted the law failed, at least morally, when confronted with the crystal of an ethic which existed both in the international community and in the USA.

6. Physiological-psychological justification: Is humanity truly free to act ethically?

Personal background: I was forced to consider various difficult questions of epistemology and the latest research in astrophysics and microbiology for my book "Does God Exist? An Answer for Today" (1978, engl. 1980), where these matters were discussed in a separate chapter. In 1994 I held a colloquium over one semester with a colleague from the Physics Institute in Tübingen on "Our Cosmos. Scientific and Philosophical-Theological Aspects" where I was able to test my views. The occasion which prompted me to reconsider central questions of cosmology, biology, and anthropology was an invitation by the Society of German Natural Scientists and Medical Doctors to give a keynote speech at their 123rd Annual Meeting in Passau on September 19, 2004. It encouraged me to present my deliberations on science and religion to a larger public in the form of five lectures in a general lecture series held in the summer semester of 2005 and subsequently published under the title "The Beginning of All Things. Science and Religion" (2005, engl. 2007). In the fifth lecture, prompted by the latest controversies, I discussed the consequences and limitations of neurological research into the brain.

(1) *Without a brain, there would be no spirit and without the activity of certain brain centers there would be no mental activity*

The brain's grey matter with its crevices and folds is a many-layered structure with functional areas containing more than ten billion neurons connected by billions of synapses and axons, connective fibers extending hundreds of thousands of kilometers. We are indebted to neuroscience for many exciting discoveries made in the last few years. With the help of functional magnetic resonance imaging, these new neuroimaging procedures have correlated various states of consciousness with certain activities occurring in specific areas of the brain. But we are only aware of the nerves connected to the cerebral cortex, and that only to a very limited extent; processes occurring outside the cortex occur unconsciously.

All psychological occurrences are closely connected to electro-chemical impulses between the neurons in the brain, and these function in accordance with the natural laws of physics. Is free will therefore an illusion? Is ethical behavior, which presumes such freedom and responsibility, therefore, in the final instance, impossible?

Neuroscientists are discovering more and more correspondences between certain states of consciousness or conscious occurrences with activities in specific (macroscopically identifiable) areas of the brain, or alternatively in (microscopic) neuronal circuits that form various areas of the brain. Some scientists have concluded from this that all our intentions, decisions, ideas, and wishes are determined by physiological processes. Everything is controlled by the unconscious, by the limbic system, which already determines in childhood, for example, whether a person will likely become a sex offender or not. This view raises the question about the consequences of such neurophysiological findings for ethics.

(2) A neuroscientific minimization of responsibility and guilt is indefensible

Criminal law, of course, acknowledges and accepts a plea of diminished responsibility. But is mental activity in principle merely an epiphenomenon of neuronal activity? Just think about it. What a *pseudo exoneration* this neuroscientific hypothesis would be for a criminal: Don't feel guilty—all of that is merely an illusion!

Sadly, neuroscientific hypotheses which declare our image of ourselves as free human beings to be mere self-deception are also responsible for the fact that neurology, which has made incredible progress using imaging, does not only raise the hope of being able to fight serious diseases such as Alzheimer's, Parkinson's, schizophrenia, depression, and recovering autonomy and freedom of choice. It also nurtures fears that humans are merely cold biological automatons. Controlled by neurons, we could be subjected to all sorts of consciousness-manipulating interventions, thereby losing our identity and autonomy. But some neurologists have also objected to this apparent neuroscientific alibi which appears to absolve humans of guilt and responsibility.

(3) Neuroscience does not currently offer any empirically verifiable theory about the relationship between the spirit and the brain

In 2004 eleven German neuroscientists published a "Manifesto on the Present State and the Future of Neuroscience." New methods have resulted in important progress, both at the *highest* level with regard to the functions of and the interactions between large areas in the brain (understanding language, recognizing pictures, perceiving sounds, processing music, planning actions, processing memories, and experiencing emotions), and at the *lowest* level with regard to what occurs at the level of individual cells and molecules (the sequence of intracellular signaling processes, the development and transmission of neuronal excitation).

But our ignorance about the all-important middle level of brain activities is still great. This is the level which permits ideas and emotions, intentions and effects, consciousness and self-aware-ness to materialize: the rules which determine how the brain works; how it depicts the world in such a way that immediate perception and previous experience are fused together; how these interior actions are experienced as our own activity and how it plans future activities. We barely understand even the rudiments of all of this.

Neuroscientists have shown themselves to be reticent with regard to the big questions: how our experience of ourselves and our consciousness is created, how rational and emotional actions are linked together, and whether our idea of free will holds water. For that, we would have to know a lot more about how the brain functions. At present, neuroscience offers no empirically verifiable theory about the relationship between consciousness and our nervous system.

(4) Neuroscience cannot answer the question about free or unfree will

The relationship between scientific theories and their objects is similar to that between a magnifying lens and the objects it is used to study: both single out certain aspects of reality while blurring some and completely ignoring others. And that is also the case with neuroscience. By placing the human spirit under the microscope, in a manner of speaking, we are also subjecting it to a specific interpretation: namely, that states of consciousness which occurred at an earlier point in time determine its later actions. This conclusion of a causality based on a succession of events is part of the chosen method. But this ignores the fact, firstly, that we might have deliberately influenced these earlier states, and secondly, that the subsequent states might have occurred spontaneously and may not have been compelled by what went before. In brief: our self-giving consciousness does not fit into the cause-and-effect scheme posited by neuroscience. It is not visualized in MRI scans and cannot be made visible using this procedure. The freedom of our consciousness can thus be real without it being possible to ascertain it experimentally.

I would like to call on three key witnesses in support of this statement:

The Tübingen behavioral neurobiologist *Niels Birbaumer* is right: "Neither free nor unfree will can be observed, because we are not acquainted with any neuronal correlative of freedom. While freedom is also a construct of the brain like all behaviors and mental activities by human beings, it is also, and primarily, a historical, political, and social phenomenon which cannot be ascribed to processes of the brain alone."

The philosopher *Peter Bieri* (Berlin) holds the purported empirical refutation of free will to be "a piece of preposterous metaphysics." "When looking at the material embodiment of a painting, you will search in vain for what it represents or for beauty, and similarly when looking at the neurobiological mechanism of the brain, you will search in vain for freedom or unfreedom. *Neither* freedom *nor* unfreedom exists there. The brain is the wrong logical place for this idea... Our will is free when it submits to our judgment about what it is right to will. Our will is unfree when judgment and will diverge..."

Following Peter Bieri, the philosopher *Jürgen Habermas* differentiates sharply between cause and reasons: "A person who acts under the causal constraint of an imposed restriction," who is thus subject to a *compelling cause*, is indeed unfree. But a person who succumbs to the "unforced force of the better argument" and who then decides to act based on *reason* is free. The bending of an arm or a finger induced by an experimenter cannot be considered a free action in the sense of moral responsibility. A free action is always the result of a complex chain of carefully considered deliberations about the goal and the means, the resources, and the obstacles. Communication between human beings, an area which was always central for Habermas as the great proponent of discourse ethics, is not the result of blind natural forces, which occur quasi behind the subject's back. Already in newborns, the human spirit only develops in the social cooperation through reciprocal influences (interactions), cooperation, and teaching. Thus the human spirit does not reside in the brain alone but is incorporated in the whole of the human person. The ego may be a social construct but that does not mean it is an illusion.

(5) *Freedom of the will can be experienced*

In their own everyday understanding of their self, neurologists constantly assume that they are responsible initiators, and they assume the same for their colleagues and patients. To declare that this self-concept is simply an epiphenomenon reveals a questionable determinist dogmatism. The laboratory perspective needs to be complemented by the perspective from the external living world; the external and internal views need to be fused. Neurologists also promise things to someone; they also declare that, regardless of the state of their brain tomorrow, they will carry out certain matters! They are thus giving themselves a degree of freedom which, according to their theories, they do not actually possess.

In addition to neurophysiological methods, the importance of introspection should not be underestimated. In fact, neurophysiologists must also constantly use introspection when they wish to interpret images and detect processes. They too must look inside themselves instead of into the MRI scanner: introspection, which can be carried out by every human being assisted by their observation of the behavior of others is capable of not only looking back. It can also grasp psychological events as they occur.

The individual repeatedly experiences others and himself as unpredictable because they are free. While the acts of a person viewed *ex post* appear to be determined, the question of what a person will do posed *ex ante* is often unanswerable. Everyone who battles with himself when making important decisions knows what I am referring to. It would be a wrong conclusion to posit from the self's construction of psychologically meaningful connections (I am doing this because, based on what has happened before, it appears to make sense) that this is an external construction determined by external physical constraints (given the facts of the matter, he could only decide in such and such a manner). This is borne out by our everyday experiences.

Persons often say no when we expect to hear a yes, and yes when we fear to hear a no. That is why election prognoses and market forecasts—even though people all too often succumb to a herd instinct—are so often disproved. I experience that within myself as an incontrovertible fact: however much I am dependent externally and internally and determined in my existence, I am still aware that, at the end of the day, this or that action still depends on me, and I choose whether I wish to talk or to keep silent in a particular situation, whether I will stand or sit, whether I prefer coffee or tea, this item of clothing or that, this journey or that. My brain may decide spontaneously that my eyes will look at someone or my foot will avoid an obstacle. However, as soon as it is a question of longer-term processes and not, as in neuroscientific experiments, of brief physical occurrences (such as the lifting of an arm or a finger)—longer-term processes which require reflection on my part, for example, the choice of career, the choice of a life partner, the purchase of a house—I need to consider opposing ideas and alternative choices of action. I must make a decision and, depending on the circumstances, I may have to correct my decision. My entire life history is also in the frame.

The developmental biologist *Alfred Gierer*, another colleague from Tübingen, was right when, in addition to neurophysiology and introspection, he emphasized the importance of willed acts as a third approach to our consciousness and our freedom: "To use the terms of information theory, the objective analysis of processes which occur in the brain can only yield some information about the states and processes of consciousness; the intersubjective transmission of conscious experience through language opens up more, willed acts yet more. All three approaches complement each other to a certain extent, but even taken together they still do not provide the full picture."

Freedom thus involves the experience not merely of thinking and feeling but also of doing. But it also includes the experience of non-doing, of failure and of guilt. In the performance or nonperformance of an act, I can directly experience its negative correlation: I didn't do it but I should have done it; I gave my promise but did not keep it; I am to blame. Why do we fret over this? Have we simply not understood the determinism which controls our actions, or in our sorrow over our acts or non-acts, do we perhaps understand our own freedom much better than those who dispute it? I acknowledge my fault and my guilt and apologize. But I also demand that the other acknowledges his fault if I was not at fault.

(6) The necessity for an ethic among scholars and scientists

Where would morality be without responsibility, where would responsibility be without freedom, where would freedom be without commitment? In an age threatened by a lack of orientation, by insecurity and pointlessness, these questions must be taken very seriously—for the sake of the humanity of human beings which is under threat and needs to be buttressed. It is crucial that we understand responsibility not as a negative barrier to freedom, but as the positive determinant of our freedom, as something which does not negate our freedom but makes it manifest, does not minimize it but realizes it. Freedom is never simply handed to us—it is mandated on us. It can only be consummated through and with responsibility. Freedom without responsibility is unfree and makes captives of us.

After the numerous scandals, big and small, which occurred over the past few years, we have been forced to acknowledge that even among scholars and scientists there are increasing numbers of cases where we see "presumption and excess, even lies and deception." And these cases must be confronted —in this matter I share the opinion of the German philosopher *Jürgen Mittelstrass*, who pointed this out quite early on (in the *Neue Zürcher Zeitung*, on July 6, 2002)—not in the first instance by "formulating an ethic for the sciences and the world of scholarship" but through reflecting on the "ideas of a universal civic ethic." That is another way of describing a global ethic.

What Mittelstrass said about science and scholarship (including the natural sciences and medicine) can be applied analogously to the economy and other areas in society: "All rules, all norms, one might wish to enforce upon scientific practice in order to strengthen its responsibilities and ensure its rationality would be futile if there were no such scientific ethic. That in reality, it is corrupt, as instances of lies and deception in scientific practice have repeatedly demonstrated, does not mean that the scientific ethic has failed or that it needs to be defined in yet more detail, but that the norms of a general ethic, of a civic ethic, have been violated and that the scientists' ethic was suspended for personal reasons." It would be important to acknowledge and observe "the basic principle of honesty towards oneself and others which applies to all sciences and disciplines." "The diagnosed crisis of credibility" is also a "crisis of ethic." "Initially, the important thing will be to remind scientists and scholars of the existence of a scientific ethic." This concerns "the implicit knowledge of the direction to be taken and the norms to be followed, and does not require a theoretical command of the subject but its practical implementation" (ibid; cf. *Wissenschaft und Weltethos* [*Science and a Global Ethic*], 1998).

7. Justification based on the study of religions: Do the religions have a similar ethic?

Personal background: Some experiences and insights go back a long time. In April 1967 I was invited in my capacity as a theologian to give a lecture at the celebration of the 100th anniversary of the American University in Beirut. By then it was clear to all persons with any knowledge or understanding of the situation that the Christian sovereignty in Lebanon was being challenged by the aggression of the Muslim population. I remain convinced of one fact up to the present day: if an attempt had been made at the time to start a serious religious dialogue between Christians and Muslims, a religious understanding could have served as a basis for a sensible and just political solution. It would have been possible to avert the civil war and the immense bloodletting.

In the 1970s I initially concentrated on the foundations of the Christian faith: I addressed questions about God, being a Christian, and eternal life. But in the 1980s I started a public dialogue at Tübingen University with specialists for Islam, Judaism, Hinduism, Buddhism, and Chinese religion. Since then I have been convinced that there can be no global peace without peace between religions, and no peace between religions without dialogue between religions, which in turn must be based on sound and in-depth research into the religions and their philosophies. But at the same time, in these dialogues I found that in matters of practical behavior, of ethics, the religions were more similar to each other than in matters of belief, of dogma. "No global peace without a peace between religions" was therefore the title of my keynote lecture at the UNESCO symposium in Paris in February 1989, in which for the first time representatives from the world religions actively took part. "Why we need global ethical standards to survive" was the title of the plenary lecture I held at the World Economic Forum in Davos in February 1990. I subsequently discussed and tested these questions during a public debate with the philosophers Hans Jonas and Karl-Otto Apel in Kiel.

The colleagues who had conducted the public dialogue between the religions with me in Tübingen also helped when in 1992 I received a request from the Council of the Parliament of the World's Religions in Chicago to draw up a declaration on a global ethic for the 1993 convention. I myself had previously proposed creating such a declaration in a lecture held in the great Rockefeller Chapel of the University of Chicago. My thoughts about the contents of such a declaration increasingly crystallized as I worked on the declaration. After reviewing the possibilities of basic trust and a straightforward ethic for believers and nonbelievers from the standpoint of philosophy, I believed this was the path through which we could arrive at a common ethic for humanity: through the world's religions to a global ethic.

The fact that the "Declaration Toward a Global Ethic" of September 4, 1993—three years after the book "Global Responsibility"—was signed by the formal delegates among the more than 6,000 participants of the Parliament of the World's Religions, first and foremost among them the Dalai Lama, greatly encouraged me and all those who had contributed to the Declaration. A mere two years later, the Global Ethic Foundation was established which took the Global Ethic Declaration of Chicago as its Magna Carta.

What followed was two decades of intensive research with many publications on the great religions of the world and their common ethic: my sweeping trilogy on Judaism (1991, engl. 1992), Christianity (1994, engl. 1995) and Islam (2004, engl. 2007) (more than 2,800 pages in total!), which was subsequently expanded by Stephan Schlensog's volume "Der Hinduismus" [Hinduism] (2006). Since the mid-1990s the work on a global ethic took the form of an extensive multimedia project "Tracing the Way. On the Trails of the World Religions:" seven films on indigenous religions, Hinduism, Chinese religion, Buddhism, Judaism, Christianity, and Islam, accompanied by a textbook (1999) and an interactive CD-ROM.

The findings unearthed there were tested repeatedly during many trips all over the world, in innumerable conversations, at interreligious events, and were confirmed by scholars and believers of various religions and so were expanded more and more over the years. What I have presented, demonstrated, and argued for in these many publications cannot be reproduced here, even rudimentarily. I can only briefly summarize it by listing three key points: world peace, world religions, and a global ethic.

(1) World peace: the new paradigm for international relationships

After two world wars, the goal of world peace required a new paradigm for international relationships, one which was indicated by the creation of the United Nations (1945) and the proclamation of the Universal Declaration of Human Rights (1948). I have sketched the emergence of this new paradigm for international relationships in books such as *Global Responsibility* (1990/1991) and *A Global Ethic for Global Politics and Economics* (1997). Many of the ideas which I covered there were subsequently included in the manifesto presented to the United Nations "Crossing the Divide" (2001). Together with the former President of the Federal Republic of Germany, Richard von Weizsäcker, I was one of twenty members of a "Group of Eminent Persons" appointed by Kofi Annan to put together a report on the dialogue between cultures and work on a new paradigm for international relationships. We presented our manifesto entitled "Crossing the Divide" to the UN Secretary-General and the UN General Assembly on November 9, 2001.

The new paradigm basically states that instead of modern power politics, national politics, politics by special interest groups, and status-driven politics, we need a politics of regional understanding, rapprochement, and reconciliation. France and Germany have shown how this can be accomplished. It requires concrete political action—also in the Middle East, Afghanistan, and Kashmir—and mutual *cooperation, compromise, and integration* instead of the previous confrontational politics, aggression, and revenge.

This new political situation clearly requires a change in mentality which needs to go far beyond the demands of day-to-day politics:

- New organizations are not sufficient for this; a new mindset is required.

- National, ethnic, or religious differences should no longer be categorically perceived as a threat but as a potential enrichment.

- While the old paradigm always presupposed an enemy, even a hereditary enemy, the new paradigm does not require an enemy anymore—but it does require partners, competitors, and often even opponents. Instead of military confrontation, there can be economic competition at all levels.

- It has been demonstrated that in the long run, national well-being cannot be promoted through war but only through peace, not through working against each other or alongside each other but by working together. And because opposing interests can be satisfied by working together, even though interests will always differ, it is possible to have a politics which is no longer a zero-sum game where one party stands to gain at the expense of the other. Instead, we are looking at a politics which is a positive-sum game: everyone wins in the end.

(2) *The world's religions: using their potential for peace rather than their potential for conflict*

For centuries, any reconciliation between the religions was impossible. The divide between the religions was too great; the ignorance, prejudice, and mistrust regarding each other ran too deep. The religions existed in a state of volitional isolation from each other. But the global situation has drastically changed.

Global politics, a global economy, and a global financial system significantly affect our own national and regional destinies. People everywhere are gradually realizing that national or regional islands of stability no longer exist. And despite the strong differences in national and regional interests we are facing an increasingly strong political, economic, and financial global integration, such that decades ago economists began referring to a *global society* and sociologists to a *global civilization* (in a technical, economic, and social sense): a global society and global civilization as interrelated areas of interaction in which we are all involved directly or indirectly. Nowadays everyone speaks of an increasingly globalized world as a matter of course.

But this emerging global society and global technological civilization do not by any means imply a uniform *global culture* (in the spiritual, artistic, and creative sense) or even a single *global religion*. In fact, a global society and a global civilization include a multitude of cultures and religions with a new focus on the wide range of cultures and religions. To hope for a single global religion is an illusion—to fear the emergence of a single global religion is nonsense. In the world of today we are still looking at a bewildering multitude of religions, denominations, religious sects, religious groups, and movements: a vast assemblage of coexisting, confused, and opposing beliefs which cannot and should not be reduced to a single common denominator.

And yet the religions do have beliefs in common. All religions—however confusingly different they may be—are messages of salvation which give an answer to similar key questions of humanity, to the eternal questions regarding love and suffering, guilt and atonement, life and death: Whence comes this world and how is it ordered? Why were we born and why must we die? What determines the fate of individuals and humanity? On what are moral consciousness and the existence of ethical norms founded? All religions also offer, over and above their interpretation of the world, similar paths to salvation. They offer paths out of misery, out of suffering, and out of the guilt of being; directions for meaningful and responsible action in this life—for lasting, abiding, eternal salvation; deliverance from all suffering, guilt, and death. The theologian *Hermann Häring* successfully summed this up in his statement "religions are the central agencies for morality in the world and as such they are indispensable."

There is no question about it: because it is a human phenomenon every religion is *ambivalent*—ambivalent like the law, the performing arts, or music, all of which have been and continue to be severely misused and abused because sociologically religions are power-hungry systems intent on the stabilization and expansion of their power. They have a high potential for conflict. But they also have an often-ignored potential for peace. Religion can stir emotions, that is true; but religion can also placate and soothe. Religion can provide the motivation for wars, fuel, and extend them, but it can also prevent and shorten wars. With the current focus on strategic, economic, and political aspects, we should not ignore the social, moral, and religious dimensions of international crises.

With an inherent potential to fuel conflict, it is not rare for religions to be exploited for the purposes of maintaining the power of certain groups. Often religion does not lie at the core of a conflict but is subsequently used by politics and society for their own purposes. There is no other way to understand the conflicts between the Balkan states. But religious communities and religious leaders, in particular, must guard against unilateral partisanship and accept their special responsibility. They should awaken an understanding within their own ambit for the other side. Religions should not unilaterally identify with a particular ethnic group or nation but act as a mediating and uniting force across the borders between ethnicities and nations.

Competing and often contradictory systems of thought and belief have developed from all of the great world religions. But peace and justice are at the heart of all religious messages. And therefore in these times, the primary task of religions must be to promote peace amongst each other, using all means now available in the media. Specifically, this means:

- clearing away misunderstandings,

- dealing with traumatic memories,

- dispelling prejudices and stereotypically negative images of the enemy,

- dealing with conflicts based on feelings of guilt within society and the individual,

- reducing hatred and destructiveness,

- recollecting what religions have in common and reflecting on humane values,

- initiating specific acts of reconciliation.

In this way, religions could help to defuse current and future conflicts centering on the unequal distribution of wealth, finite resources and water, or the consequences of climate change. Of course, religion cannot be responsible for resolving all of the world's problems. But religion can help politics, the economy, and culture become more sensitive to problems and also provide assistance that will allow uncomfortable solutions to prevail. Recent studies have shown that religions and religious communities have their own special means of non-escalating or de-escalating political conflicts and promoting peace. These special means include the prevention of violence, human rights work, public statements, nonviolent resistance, good offices, mediation, and even the assumption for a brief time of political offices and functions.

With regard to the promotion of peace, religions are often rated disparately and judged unfairly: in the West Christianity is often considered an ally of human rights and the rule of law. In contrast, Islam is considered a wellspring of terrorism and fundamentalist violence. At best it is conceded that Christian fundamentalism did exist in the past (Crusades) but that this misinterpretation of Christianity has since been overcome.

Every religion has its own history and merits a differentiated appraisal. As a Christian one should not be blind to the failures of the church in the past. The rule of law and human rights were largely enforced in the teeth of fierce opposition on the part of the churches. In the Catholic Church, human rights have only been recognized since Pope John XXIII and the Second Vatican Council. As with Christianity, we must allow other religions to go through a learning process where they correct their mistakes themselves and have their missteps corrected by others. Everyone needs to first remove the log in their own eye before tackling the speck in their neighbor's eye.

The following must always hold true: treating people humanely is the minimum requirement for every religion. Conversely—it is a dialectical reciprocal relationship— religion, understood correctly, offers optimal conditions to realize the principle of treating people humanely. Christian charity, as described in the New Testament, does not devalue humaneness but deepens and radicalizes it (e.g. human charity and loving your enemies).

A trilateral methodology like I used in my three books *Judaism*, *Christianity*, and *Islam* can help promote an equitable and fair appraisal, in particular of the three related Abrahamic religions Judaism, Christianity, and Islam: the description and criticism of the individual religions are constantly interlaced with a criticism or self-criticism of the other religions. This resulted in an external dialogic and a conceptual interlocking of the trilogy.

My decades-old preoccupation with the great world religions has nurtured my conviction that every religion has a powerful potential for peace. And this potential is particularly rooted in an ethic.

(3) A global ethic: observing common ethical standards despite huge dogmatic differences

Firstly: As previously mentioned, an understanding between religions does not aim to draw up battle lines between believers and nonbelievers. The Roman Catholic re-catholicing campaign, particularly strong in Eastern Europe and euphemistically termed re-evangelization, does not offer a role model; it only reopened old wounds and deepened old conflicts. We do not need yet another partitioning of society or division of political parties into clerical and anticlerical parties. The global ethic project virtually demands an alliance between believers and nonbelievers in support of a new and shared basic ethic.

Secondly: It cannot be doubted that the religions have a particular role to play and a special responsibility with regard to the existence of a basic ethic, shared values, binding standards, and personal basic core beliefs. What unites all great religions has been examined and teased out in detail by examining source material and tradition. The religions can, if they want, emphasize the basic maxims of elementary humanity with a greater authority and conviction than politicians, jurists, and philosophers—particularly the *Rule of Humanity*, "Every human being must be treated humanely!" and the *Golden Rule of Reciprocity*, "Do unto others what you would have others do unto you."

These must enter the general consciousness: all great religions have certain "non-negotiable standards," i.e., basic ethical norms and maxims for action. These are justified with reference to the unconditional, and must, therefore, be held to be unconditionally applicable for hundreds of millions of people—even if, of course, they are not always complied within individual cases. But an ethic is always also counterfactual: in reality, an ethic will always be repeatedly contravened against. But nevertheless, there is an important difference between an ethic that still applies in principle and an ethic that has been effectively infiltrated or overridden, ousted, or forgotten: knowing oneself to be culpable when one has become culpable.

The *Declaration Toward a Global Ethic*, issued by the Parliament of the World's Religions on September 4, 1993, in Chicago, has provided concretions on this point. The declaration constituted an unparalleled step in the modern history of religions: it showed that it was possible at a gathering of people from the world's religions to agree upon a basic document that formulated shared ethical principles and unshakeable directives. All religions could and should actively support it and commit their adherents to the principles of the declaration. Below, once again, are the four unshakeable directives in a more concrete form:

- The commitment to a culture of *nonviolence* and *respect for all life*: "You shall not kill—but you shall also not torture, torment, or hurt"—or to put it positively "Have respect for life!"

- The commitment to a culture of *solidarity* and a *just economic order*: "You shall not steal—but you shall also not exploit, bribe, corrupt"—or to put it positively, "Act honestly and fairly!"

- The commitment to a culture of *tolerance* and a life of *truthfulness*: "You shall not lie—but you shall also not deceive, falsify, manipulate"—or to put it positively, "Speak and act truthfully!"

- And finally, and this is admittedly the area where all religions have the biggest problems: the commitment to a culture of *equal rights* and *partnership between men and women*: "You shall not abuse sexuality—but you shall also not abuse, humiliate, or degrade your partner"—or to put it positively, "Respect and love one another!"

In 1993, many theologians and religious scholars were surprised by this document. To others—particularly those with experience in interreligious dialogue—the idea of a global ethic was immediately plausible. For many of them, the concept was electrifying. The question which has sometimes been raised—whether the consensus formulated in the Chicago Declaration actually exists or whether it was merely theological wishful thinking on the part of interreligious idealists—can be clearly answered: Yes, this overall consensus on an ethic across religions and cultures does exist!

We can find its principles and values in the scriptures, sacred writings, and fundamental documents of the great world religions. They are a central theme of many religious and humanist traditions where they are affirmed and lived: not only in the Abrahamic religions—Judaism, Christianity, and Islam—but also in the religions which originated in Indian and in Chinese tradition. We have described this in minute detail in our work of the last twenty years, and both interested persons and skeptics can find exhaustive information in these publications. When you talk to people from these cultures and religions and ask about the attitudes and behaviors demanded by their traditions and what they adhere to in their lives, time and again you will hear these and similar principles. And these principles can also be shared by nonbelievers when they wish to assume ethical responsibility for the world and society. Nevertheless, religion should not be disregarded.

(4) The advantage of religion

As much as I esteem philosophy, when retrospectively reviewing the philosophical and scholarly arguments in favor of a global ethic it cannot be denied that, like philosophy, religion has its own particular strengths. In addition to its identified ethical function the advantage of religion is clearly demonstrated by the following points:

- More than philosophy, which with its ideas and teachings appeals at least to an intellectual elite, religion can mold and motivate broader sections of the population.

- Religion appeals to people not only at a rational level but also at an emotional level, not only through ideas, concepts, and words, but also through symbols, rites, prayers, and festivals, and thus offers additional value for human beings as a whole.

- Religions are based on ancient holy scriptures and traditions which offer normative guidelines for human behavior based on religious experience, shaping the morality of human beings in many cases for thousands of years. The traditions of religion thus buttress continuity over generations.

- Through the experiences and tales, symbols, rituals, and festivals it passes on, religion is able to create a spiritual home and community, a home of trust, belief, and certainty.

- Religious practices: both individual practices such as prayer and collective practices such as religious services can strengthen the personal self and communicate security and hope. This can give rise not merely to a feeling of togetherness but may also be a seed for protests and resistance against existing systems of injustice (nonviolent revolution with candles).

- All religions have founding or symbolic figures who did not merely proclaim the ethic but also lived it; adherents of a religion are often called upon to emulate the lives of these figures. They offer concrete ways of living which, even today, centuries or thousands of years later, can offer guidance and orientation.

III.

What Does a Global Ethic Mean in Practice?

1. Politics and a global ethic

Personal background: Since the war and from the post-war period onward, I have been passionately interested in global political events. The paradigm shift which in 1989 penetrated to socialist countries prompted me to summarize my own political convictions, which I had reviewed many times and which had matured over the years, in my book "Projekt Weltethos" 1990 ("Global Responsibility" 1991). After my historical, political, and theological studies "Judaism" (1991/1992) and "Christianity" (1994/1995), I wanted to set out, with a full awareness of history and contemporary events, how a "Global Ethic for Global Politics and Economics" (1997) can and should be promoted. Without a knowledge of history (for example of "realpolitik" ranging from

Machiavelli to Richelieu, Napoleon, Metternich, Bismarck, and Palmerston, to Hans J. Morgenthau and Henry Kissinger) it appeared to me that it would be impossible to analyze the shift from the old European to the new polycentric paradigm. It would be impossible to understand even the most basic aspects of the complex current politics.

After the fateful recidivism of the United States and its return to the old nationalist-imperialist paradigm of military confrontation under the younger President Bush (2001–2009), a commitment to a new paradigm of international relationships appeared to be more urgent than ever before. The unnecessary 10-year war in Iraq, a war waged in contravention of international conventions and against all Christian morality, had a high price: more than 5,000 dead soldiers from amongst President Bush's Coalition of the Willing, more than 100,000 dead Iraqi civilians (an investigation in 2011 counted 160,000 dead), more than one trillion dollars spent on the war, and an incalculable loss of prestige and trust in the United States by East and West.

I would like to add a few brief words of thanks here: if I could thank all those people worldwide, and particularly in the United States, who have helped me over a period of six decades to understand this world, its politics, and economy—through contacts, talks, books, during trips, at conferences, experts' meetings, during semesters spent abroad and meetings in my own house—I would fill innumerable pages.

At the latest after the Second World War, despite much overt resistance, a new post-modern paradigm of politics began to slowly and laboriously assert itself. This paradigm is no longer Eurocentric but polycentric and aims to create – post-colonially and post-imperially—a world of truly united nations. Given this development and the new era, it is clear that what is now required is not old-style geopolitical power brokers. What we need are authentic and upright state leaders such as the great state leaders of the immediate post-war period in Europe; state leaders who are highly intelligent and decisive with stamina, who also have an ethical vision and concrete concepts which they know how to implement coupled with a strong sense of responsibility.

In other words, a middle course between realpolitik and idealistic policies is possible, a course that can strike a happy medium and yet is not mediocre. It involves policies undertaken in the spirit of an ethics of responsibility as described by Max Weber and Hans Jonas. Regarding foreign policy, it is necessary to start by making two negative distinctions:

(1) No ruthless realpolitik

An ethics of success of the type propagated by the sort of politicians who favor a policy of political realism *(realpolitik)* where the political end justifies all means, even immoral ones such as lies, deception, betrayal, torture, political murder, and war, is unsuitable for a new world order. Neither the diplomatic service, the secret service, nor the police stand above morality. Machiavellianism, an attitude which only focuses on Machiavelli's amoral advice, has brought infinite suffering, blood, and tears to nations and peoples. It is not only such perpetrators of evil as Hitler and Stalin, Pol-Pot (Cambodia), and Idi Amin (Uganda). Nor should one think only of the secret police and the secret services in various countries which (take the KGB in the Soviet Union, the Stasi in the GDR, but also the CIA in the United States) plotted assassinations, committed felonies, and even successfully taught others how to blackmail, abduct, torture, and murder. Many politicians who have not acted as state leaders but as unprincipled opportunists spring to mind, politicians whose single constant guiding political principle in their domestic and foreign policy has been the advancement of their own power and the securing of their own reelection and did not deserve to be reelected. Nevertheless:

(2) But also no moralizing ethics of principle

An ethics of principle as favored by idealistic politicians is similarly unsuitable for a new world order as a moral motivation and a good cause are considered sufficient with little thought spared for the real balance of power, the feasibility of policies in practice, and possible negative consequences. In international politics, the term "well meant" often stands for "the opposite of good." Apocalypticism can wreak as much havoc as playing down and trivializing potential consequences. Indeed, worthy motives do not guarantee good policies. If a person has good intentions, they and others may believe themselves to be worthy and upright, but this is not an indication that their policies will bring good results.

Part of the art of politics is a good assessment not merely of the intended consequences, but also of incidental and unintended consequences which may be quite serious. In the final instance, a person who acts honorably but without regard to possible unpleasant consequences and incidental side effects acts irresponsibly or even culpably, even if he is content to lay the blame on others or on the circumstances when he fails. Wrongful idealism has also misled entire nations, leading them to an impracticable nowhere, to a dystopia. This does not only apply to crusades and so-called religious wars but also to modern wars between nations and ideologies. What matters are not the motives but the results, which is why institutional political ethics must be complemented by a results-oriented ethic. The positive conclusion is therefore:

(3) A middle path of accountable, responsible rationality

Only an ethics of responsibility is suitable for a new world order. Such a middle course is anything but mediocre! An ethics of responsibility requires an ethos but also realistically considers the foreseeable, in particular, the negative, consequences of certain policies and takes responsibility for them. The art of politics in the postmodern paradigm consists of convincingly combining political calculation (modern realpolitik) and ethical judgment (idealistic politics), continually balancing the two against each other and persistently searching for new ways of doing so. An ethics of responsibility, as I understand it, does not mean a modern, autonomous politics without norms nor does it mean a quasi-medieval heteronomous politics based on norms alone. I advocate a middle course of accountable, responsible rationality between two extremes.

The one extreme is irresponsible Machiavellianism and libertinism, a politics where people believe they can dispense with ethical principles, standards, and maxims in politics and in their private life; a politics which is only guided by the current continually changing situation, and decisions are determined solely based on the question at issue, purely in response to the current moment alone. According to this point of view, promises and contracts only apply *rebus sic stantibus*, i.e., as long as things are the way they are. It is entirely natural to break a contract if the situation changes. Loyalties and alliances are constantly changing.

The other extreme is irrational legalism and dogmatism, which in politics and private life simply and inflexibly adheres to the letter of the alleged divine law, unheeding of and untroubled by the specific situation (the Restoration Popes Wojtyla and Ratzinger offered good examples of this). Church policies, basic principles, standards, and maxims which were possibly eminently sensible in earlier times—whether the issue was contraception and population policies or abortion and assisted euthanasia—are considered infallible; church laws must apply unconditionally, without exception, in every situation.

(4) Instead of dogma or tactics, an accountable, responsible decision may be arrived at conscientiously

Responsibility has many dimensions: I am responsible to other people, I am responsible to myself and to my conscience, and I am responsible to God. Politicians may also face situations where Luther's statement "Here I stand, I can do no other!" applies, where in fact they must decide according to their personal conscience. In principle, an ethical imperative must always be dependent on the situation. But in certain situations it can be categorical, an obligation which is laid upon the person's conscience without any ifs, ands, or buts, not a hypothetical imperative but an unconditional one. For political ethics this means:

- Political ethics do not consist of an inflexible *doctrinaire thetic* (collection of dogmatic propositions) by dog-matists who refuse all compromise. Ethical norms that do not take the political situation into account are counterproductive; ethical decisions are always pragmatic.

- Political ethics are not crafty clever tactics by opportun-ists who come up with an excuse for everything. If a political situation is no longer measured against ethical norms, the result will be unscrupulousness. Tactical and strategic considerations taken at the expense of ethical principles may cost a politician dearly in his political life.

* Political ethics stand for an obligation laid upon one's conscience which does not focus on what is good or right in the abstract but on what is good or right in a specific concrete context, which considers what is appropriate in a specific situation and combines a general normative constant with a particular situational variable. An ethics of responsibility and an ethics of principle, both a far cry from Machiavellianism and moralizing, can go hand in hand. This is the only way in which the three preeminent qualities Max Weber demands of politicians' passion, a sense of responsibility, and a sense of proportion—will be utilized properly.

Political ethics does not refer alone to politically active individuals; it also concerns institutional and collective agents of politics, not merely at a local or national level but also at a global level.

(5) No global politics without a global ethic

Even in the "realistic" discipline of political science awareness of global ethical responsibility is growing, a responsibility which does not only apply to business leaders or ruling elites. When I published my book *Projekt Weltethos* in 1990, I was unable to find many documents by global organizations on ethical principles. The *Global Ethic Declaration of the Parliament of the World's Religions* was proclaimed in 1993, a mere three years after the publication of *Projekt Weltethos*. Four years later, when I published a realistic forward-looking overview under the title *A Global Ethic for Global Politics and Economics,* three more important documents, mentioned above, had been created. All of them, as their titles implied, demanded a global ethic and attempted to give it a more concrete form. A global ethic is indispensable in the age of globalization, and humanity has paid dearly for the fact that its political leaders have so often disregarded it. Let me only briefly point to the following documents (cf. Chapter IV):

- the report by the Commission on Global Governance appointed by the United Nations,

- the report by the World Commission on Culture and Development,

- the proposal by the InterAction Council (IAC) of former heads of state and government for a Universal Declaration of Human Responsibilities.

Already in 2000, long before the start of the global financial and economic crisis of 2008, the then head of the International Monetary Fund Dr. Horst Köhler admonished his listeners in his inaugural speech in Prague, commenting that a globalization of ethics would be required in order to cope with global problems: "Indeed, as Hans Küng has said, the global economy needs a global ethic."

My conviction remains the one given in a statement which I, as a member of a "Group of Eminent Persons" appointed by the then Secretary-General of the United Nations Kofi Annan, was privileged to present to the General Assembly of the United Nations on November 9, 2001, following the debate on the *Dialogue between Cultures.* "Faced with the current troubles and trials many people ask themselves: Will the 21st century really be better than the 20th century with its history of violence and wars? Will we really achieve a new world order, a better world order? … Our group proposes such a vision of a new paradigm for international relationships which also includes new protagonists on the global scene.

These days religions are once again making an appearance as protagonists in global politics. It is true that far too often throughout history religions have shown their destructive side. They have sown and legitimized hatred, enmity, violence, and even war. But in many cases they have sown and legitimized understanding, reconciliation, cooperation, and peace. Over the past few decades, initiatives promoting interreligious dialogue and cooperation between religions have sprung up all over the world. Through this dialogue the world's religions have once again discovered that their own fundamental ethical teachings support and deepen the secular ethical values enshrined in the Universal Declaration of Human Rights.

At the 1993 Parliament of the World's Religions in Chicago over 200 representatives from all of the world's religions declared for the first time in history their agreement with regard to certain commonly held ethical values, standards, and attitudes as a basis for a global ethic, which was then included in our report to the UN Secretary-General and the General Assembly of the United Nations…

"In this age of globalization such a global ethic is absolutely necessary: Globalization needs a global ethic not as an additional burden but as its basis, to help human beings and to promote a civil society. Some political scientists have predicted a 'clash of cultures' in the 21st century. We posit an alternative vision for the future; a vision which is not merely an optimistic ideal but which represents a realistic vision of hope: that the religions and cultures of the world, working together with all persons of goodwill, can help prevent such a clash."

The proposals of our group regarding the outline of a new paradigm for international relationships, for a future model of cooperation between cultures and religions, were later made generally available under the title *Crossing the Divide* and in many areas still await their implementation (cf. Chapter V, 5).

2. *Economics and a global ethic*

Personal background: Right from the start of the Global Ethic project, the economy—together with religions, politics, and education—was at the center of our efforts. In 1997 my book "A Global Ethic for Global Politics and Economics" came out as a follow-up to the book "Global Responsibility." After I had attended the World Economic Forum in Davos several times, I participated in the Annual Conference of the International Confederation of Stock Exchanges in Kuala Lumpur where I presented my lecture, "Ethical Standards for International Financial Transactions." Like the Global Ethic Declaration of 1993, the proposal for a Universal Declaration of Human Responsibilities put forward by the InterAction Council of former heads of state and government also includes a section about a just economic order. We tackled the topic head-on in 2001 at an international and interdisciplinary symposium held in Baden-Baden under the heading "Global Companies—A Global Ethic: the global market demands new standards and a global framework" [Globale Unternehmen—Globales Ethos] which was subsequently published as a book.

In line with all these preliminary works, a manifesto for a global economic ethic was prepared in 2009, penned by a panel of experts from the Global Ethic Foundation which included economists, entrepreneurs, and ethicists (cf. Part IV, 3). At the same time, confirmed in my opinions by the 2008 global financial and economic crisis which had by then erupted, I completely revised my 1997 publication on a global ethic and the global economy and expanded it into the book "Anständig wirtschaften. Warum Ökonomie Moral braucht" (Fair Dealings. Why the Economy Needs Morality), published in 2010. In this book, I again particularly focused on the historical developments which explained the current economic crisis. I critically queried the economic and political concept of economic ultraliberalism ("a domestication of ethics by the economy!") and the concept of a social market economy ("the new ecological and ethical challenges"). The in-depth historical review was followed by a discussion on "ways out of the crisis" together with a systematic analysis of "economic activity out of responsibility" which included practical applications. I will attempt to summarize the most important points below:

(1) Which economic and political concept? A market economy with social obligations

In the great conflict between two social, philosophical, economic, and political ideas, the market economy has clearly prevailed over the concept of a planned economy. Since then, the discussion has centered on the question, which market economy? One proposal, promoted particularly by the United States, is for an unfettered, unregulated market economy, a pure market economy (without limitations or controls).

But after the disastrous experiences of previous and current global financial and economic crises it might be difficult to convince people today of the benefits of a pure market economy. The question is now how to establish a market economy with social obligations, a social market economy. After the Second World War, one example of a social market economy was implemented in the Federal Republic of Germany, but this model is currently also in crisis as modifications to the expansive welfare state have become very necessary.

(2) Ways out of the global economic crisis: Three failed systems

- There has been a failure of the markets themselves: moral hazard, excessive financial speculation (real estate and stock market), overvalued currencies, poor timing for short-term loans, the existence of a strong black market, and a contagion effect.

- There has been a failure of the institutions: inadequate functioning of regulatory and control systems, of the banking system, the legal infrastructure and financial system, insufficient protection of property rights, a lack of transparency, and inadequate standards for balance sheets.

- There has been a failure of morality, which is at the root of the failure of the markets and institutions: crony and mafia capitalism, bribery and corruption, a lack of trust and social responsibility, and excessive greed on the part of investors or institutions (J. H. Dunning).

It should be clear that for the economy, morality and ethics are neither marginal nor artificially contrived and that it is right to use the term "moral framework" to describe the framework which interdependently and interactively links markets, governments, trade associations, and supranational organizations. An ethic is not merely a moral appeal, but it stands for moral actions.

(3) Doing business responsibly: without institutionalized greed and lies

As the Asian financial crisis of the 1990s already demonstrated, what is needed is a reorganization of the global financial system. Such a reorganization requires reflection about certain minimal ethical values, attitudes, and standards which are necessary. A global ethic for this global society and global economy is required, an ethic to which all nations and interest groups can commit themselves. Like a framework for financial markets which (similar to the Bretton Woods Agreement at the time) must have global applicability so that participants cannot simply flee to other markets when they encounter constraints, a basic ethical consensus would also have to be globally applicable to ensure a tolerably peaceful and just coexistence on our globe. Therefore:

(4) A global market economy demands a global ethic of humanity

Markets and ethics are not irreconcilably opposed worlds, but it must be clear which must take precedence (primacy)—certainly not the markets:

- Politics must always take primacy over the economy: the economy does not only exist to supply the allegedly rational, strategic, self-interested needs of "homo economicus." Politics—which look after the needs of human beings, communities, and humanity as a whole—must set the rules and the economy must adhere to them.

- At the same time, ethics must take primacy over the economy and politics. However essential the economy and politics are, they are only individual aspects in the world of human beings and must be subject to the ethical standards of humanity for the sake of humankind's humanity.

This means that neither the economy nor politics can take precedence; instead, it is important to always preserve the inviolable dignity of the human person together with the basic rights and obligations inherent to being human. A politics independent of economic interests is possible, but not politics detached from ethical norms. But what type of ethic should apply?

(5) No ethics of principle devoid of economic rationality

A mere ethics of principle as postulated by idealistic economists is not suitable for a new economic order. For economists of this sort, a purely moral motivation and a good and often noble purpose (justice, love, truthfulness, peace) is sufficient. Such economists appear to give little thought to the laws of the economy and the concrete feasibility of implementing rules within a highly complex economic system. This type of idealistic economic ethics of principle tends, from the outset, to discredit profit seeking both in principle and in concrete cases, labeling them immoral.

To this we must respond: to set up moral demands without any economic rationality for the world at large, that is, without paying any heed to economic laws, is not morality—it is moralistic determinism. Competition, the pursuit of self-interest, and profit seeking are legitimate, provided they do not violate higher goods and the rights of other people.

(6) But also no ethics of success devoid of moral principles

And similarly we must state: a mere ethics of success as propagated by realistic economists is also unsuitable for a new global economic order. For economists of this sort, profit justifies all means, if necessary even immoral means such as breaches of trust, lies, deceit, and unrestrained rapacity. This elevates morally justified profit seeking to the status of a dogmatic profit principle or even a profit maximization principle.

To this we must respond: to argue in favor of dogmatic economic views without ethical norms is not economics but economic reductionism, economic determinism. On no account must primacy be accorded exclusively to success. The pursuit of one's own interest and all forms of entrepreneurship must, in the final instance, also take ethical responsibility, even if in specific cases of economic competition this may appear to be an imposition.

And here then is the positive answer: only actions by realistic economists with an idealistic outlook based on an ethic of responsibility are suitable for a new global economic order. Such an ethic requires a self-commitment to one's own conscience and values in business; inquires realistically about foreseeable consequences, in particular the negative consequences of economic decisions; and assumes responsibility for them. To make the right decision while following the dictates of one's conscience presupposes the availability of information and a capacity for self-criticism. Because of the uncertainty which always remains, the decision may be taken based on intuition, although it will not necessarily be irrational.

Accountable, responsible economic activity in our times therefore consists of convincingly combining economic strategies and ethical judgment. This new paradigm of an economic ethic finds its concrete expression in examining economic activities—in spite of the natural striving to maximize profits—with an eye to whether these activities violate a higher good or more important values, whether they are socially compatible and environmentally sustainable for the future; in short, whether they are truly humane and humanitarian.

(7) Commitment to an ethical corporate culture

Let us now turn our gaze from the global economy and look at the corporate level. Nowadays we expect corporate management to be competent in three quite different areas, all of which will vary according to the size of the company. They need to be

- economically competent with regard to markets, the company, and individuals;

- politically competent with regard to institutions, which are responsible at local, regional, and national levels, and international organizations;

- ethically competent with regard to their own personality and character. An entrepreneur or a manager must not only think strategically but must also exemplify in his or her own behavior what he or she expects of others. In the end, it comes down to the individual which spirit will prevail within a company.

A good and ethically informed corporate culture does not happen by itself. The company has to actively promote it—and must continue to promote it—time and again. It is not enough to print glossy brochures detailing guidelines and corporate goals and assume that these guidelines will be implemented and that this will be enough to satisfy any obligation to act responsibly. A culture of values can only develop in an atmosphere of trust, and that, in turn, is the basis for fairness and loyalty. In concrete terms, this means:

Firstly: *Compliance*, i.e., observing laws, is quite rightly the basic requirement for corporate culture today. Fraud, manipulation, and corruption have occurred and still occur even in well-known companies in Western countries. Without a sense of integrity and a real appreciation of values such as truthfulness and justice— values which must be promoted at all corporate levels—it is unlikely that there will be any long-term improvement.

Secondly: The fact that more and more companies are openly professing their social responsibility, their *corporate social responsibility*, is a welcome development. But it is not rare for this avowed commitment to social goals to be limited to selected social, cultural, or environmental initiatives. True social responsibility goes far beyond that. It involves the entire business operations of a company, its employees, and all those affected by the company. It rests on the awareness of values such as responsibility, humanity, and solidarity, values which are the foundations of a truly responsible corporate culture.

Thirdly: Over the past few years, innumerable companies have developed elaborate mission statements, implemented structures, created institutions, and issued documents. But often this has resulted in little change to the corporate culture. Mission statements need a foundation. They require a *readiness by all persons involved* to implement these mission statements in daily corporate life. The mission statements should correspond to the *attitudes* of those people for whom they are intended. For this reason it is necessary to talk about these attitudes (virtues); ethical convictions and values must be discussed openly and honestly in the boardroom, and above all, these values must be lived.

Senior management has a special role to play. Passing on values is always a top-down process which needs to start at the top if the values are to percolate down to the bottom. As in education, the passing on of values within a company can only be sustained by *role models*. Values must be lived and exemplified by the management and by those in positions of responsibility. Values must be communicated within the company and they must be experienced by employees. It is obvious that such processes succeed best in flat hierarchies and within small units, among employees who are well qualified and motivated. The larger, more complex, and anonymous the structure, the more difficult such processes will be.

However, in all companies the *selection criteria* and *promotion practices* for management personnel play an important role. Whether employees with ethical convictions, emotional intelligence, and social skills are promoted to executive positions does not merely directly impact the decisions taken in these companies and their respective policies. It also has a signal effect that should not be underrated within the company itself and far beyond the company. The question which has often been posited by critics, whether *successful business practices and ethical convictions* are compatible with each other, can be answered with a resounding yes with reference to examples that exist in many companies. In today's time of crisis the new future generation of leaders and top executives—this is borne out by examples at universities and business schools worldwide—is much more open to considering ethical questions as part of the larger picture than many of their teachers, some of whom still adhere to old paradigms, are prepared to acknowledge.

(8) Manifesto for a global economic ethic

This manifesto (www.globaleconomicethic.org) succinctly summarizes the key points of a global economic ethic. The two principles of the Declaration Toward a Global Ethic of 1993—the Principle of Humanity and the Rule of Reciprocity—also form the basis (Part I) of the new manifesto (Art. 1-4). As in the Global Ethic Declaration, the four imperatives in the manifesto—which have already been discussed elsewhere—are based on the Principle of Humanity and the Rule of Reciprocity. These imperatives are not to kill (cf. Art. 5-6), not to steal (cf. Art. 7-9), not to lie (cf. Art. 10-11), and not to abuse sexuality (cf. Art. 12-13).

So what is special about this manifesto? Numerous quite useful ethic declarations, Codes of Conduct, or company mission statements already exist today. The manifesto is not intended as a replacement for them. Instead, the manifesto provides a norm, a standard against which company practice and company aims defined in the company's code of conduct can be measured. Two aspects illustrate what characterizes our manifesto:

1. The manifesto firstly demonstrates the *continuity* of certain values and standards over time, an endurance which continues to hold good despite upheavals and changes. These values and standards are backed by the authority of the great religious and ethical traditions of humanity as reflected in innumerable testimonies from different cultures passed down over centuries. They are therefore no invention of our time but taken from the ethical treasure trove of humanity's experience which has accumulated since humankind, ascending from the animals, first had to learn to behave truly humanly, to behave humanely! We had to learn, for example, that other people cannot be killed in the

same way that human beings—of course not unlimitedly!—are permitted to kill animals.

2. Our manifesto for a global economic ethic demonstrates secondly that these values and norms *are universally present across all regions*. Despite being obviously culturally dependent this universal presence is by no means fortuitous—how so? As we have heard, human beings in all cultures have always accorded particular protection to life, property, honor, and sexuality.

Thus, the values and norms given in the manifesto have not been chosen arbitrarily. Nonviolence and respect for life, justice and solidarity, truthfulness and tolerance, mutual respect, and partnership are part of the foundations in core areas of life.

The manifesto not only lays down certain general formal moral rules or postulates, such as responsibility or public weal, but also looks at the content of certain values and ethical standards. The manifesto is not a law that needs to be enforced with sanctions; it is an appeal to commit oneself, an appeal subject to the sanctions of the person's own conscience. This appeal is not merely aimed at economic leaders, entrepreneurs, and investors but at loan creditors, employees, customers, consumers, and interest groups in all countries all over the world. Thus it is also aimed at political, state, and international organizations and institutions, all of which have an important responsibility for the development and implementation of a global economic ethic.

In his foreword to the German/English printed version of the manifesto, the well-known American economist Professor Jeffrey Sachs, Director of the Earth Institute at Columbia University (New York) strongly espoused the new economic paradigm and manifesto for a global economic ethic, writing: "The chronic lack of attention to the world's poor, and the shoddy business practices of many of the world's leading companies, is joined by a third moral blight of our time: the failure to take effective decisions to protect the physical earth from degradation caused by unguided natural resource use." He continues: "These are all certainly problems of institutions, organization, technology, and public understanding. But as Hans Küng, Klaus Leisinger, and Josef Wieland make brilliantly clear, they are also problems of moral agency. Ethical standards are needed to harness public understanding and action, and those ethical standards need to be embraced by business leaders acting within and on behalf of private companies, politicians acting as chosen representatives of collective action, and citizens acting as members of a now global community, and as the current trustees of a planet that will be home for countless generations to come."

3. A global ethic as a "pedagogical" project (Stephan Schlensog)

(1) Learning to live with each other

"We simply have to learn to live with each other!" This urgent appeal was voiced at the end of a radio discussion between the philosophers Hans Martin Schönherr-Mann and Hans-Georg Gadamer. Gadamer is said to have exhaustedly whispered this sentence in an almost imploring voice into the studio microphone at the end of a lengthy and intense philosophical discussion—to all intents and purposes it represents the quintessence of his concerns. In simple words and in a nutshell, without complex philosophical theories: "We simply have to learn to live with each other!" Professor Schönherr-Mann later used part of this quotation for the title of a book on modern philosophy and the battle between cultures in which he presented numerous, often surprising references from modern thinkers on the topic of a global ethic. Hans Küng has discussed some of these viewpoints in his comments on the philosophical justification of a global ethic.

Learn to live with each other: When we encounter others, they must be treated with esteem and respect, with the willingness, despite all the differences between people, to search for ways of successfully cooperating together. But such cooperation will not automatically succeed or happen by itself. It is necessary to carefully consider the preconditions and foundations for such cooperation. Good and successful cooperation must be learned and requires continual practice for it to be perpetuated and effective. And therefore learning to live with each other means *living together successfully as part of a learning process, as a pedagogical project*. This is yet another way of paraphrasing the aims of the global ethic project. The task of the Global Ethic Foundation is to transpose these aims into people's daily lives and provide answers to different challenges human beings face today.

(2) *Learning to understand other cultures*

The global ethic idea developed against the background of great global political change. By the end of the 1980s Hans Küng believed that the most important future challenges facing human-ity were no longer the confrontation between geopolitical blocks and major ideologies in East and West. Conflicts threatened all along cultural and religious borders: not merely along the divide between the Western world and the Islamic world but also within continents and nations, in people's heads and hearts. To be able to defuse these conflicts, perhaps even prevent them, and to calm burgeoning tensions as early as possible, it is necessary to know more about one another. It is necessary to meet with one another face-to-face in an atmosphere of mutual respect; it is necessary to maintain a critical dialogue. All of this is not merely necessary, in Küng's opinion at the time and in our opinion and based on our experience today, it is also possible.

At the time Hans Küng strongly disagreed with the American political scientist Samuel Huntington. With his prognosis of an unavoidable future clash of cultures Huntington made a name for himself all over the world and, particularly after the attacks of September 11, 2001, he was offering an apparently plausible interpretation for such a previously unthinkable catastrophe. Huntington ignored the fact that all over the globe millions of people were living peacefully together despite their different religions and cultures. According to Huntington's pessimistic vision, intercultural conflicts, possibly even a large-scale global conflict between Islam (in coalition with the Chinese!) and the Western world are inescapable and bound to occur.

Hans Küng's slogan of "No global peace without peace between religions" which summarizes his agenda does not refuse to acknowledge the potential for conflict between religions and cultures. Quite the contrary. But with his concept of a global ethic Hans Küng draws the opposite conclusions. And in formulating this idea he has expressed what many people feel.

What is described here at a global level as a global challenge is mirrored today on a smaller scale in virtually all countries and societies. All societies, whether they want to or not, now face the challenge of organizing the coexistence of people from different cultures, ethnic groups, beliefs, and worldviews. Totalitarian systems, whether secular or religious, which attempt to repress this pluralism—sometimes even through violence—will not prevail, given the rapid advance of globalization and the increasing global integration of transportation, communication, and business in our time.

But let us not look at others—let us examine ourselves. Even in a country like Germany, the idea of a multicultural society has been a constant issue for years—not merely since the September 2001 attacks. Tensions and conflicts, both big and small, constantly recur in our country when worlds literally collide, as people from different cultures and life situations meet. Think of the public discussions about whether certain religions have the capacity for democracy, of the controversies about caricatures of the Prophet Mohammed, of reports on problem schools and problem areas in our cities, of the discussions about building mosques and minarets, and much else besides.

And by 2015 at the latest, when hundreds of thousands of refugees fleeing the warzones of Syria and Iraq and immigrants from North Africa sought refuge in Europe, it was once again demonstrated that now, more than ever, flows of refugees are a global political fact whether the streams of refugees are caused by war, the deepening fault lines in the global economy, or climate change. If security and prosperity will not come to people, then people will continue to move where they can find security and prosperity.

So the subject of immigrants remains a hot topic in many countries—in politics, in the media, and in local pubs—an issue which continues to be debated hotly or calmly. Such debates rarely offer solutions—not least because the problems, when examined with a clear eye, are extremely complex and because the people who often vociferously proclaim their opinions during such discussion seldom do justice to the complexity of the issue.

Of course, this is only one side of the story. In many countries there are also numerous places where multicultural coexistence works well. And there are many institutions, associations, initiatives, and individuals who help to ensure that multicultural coexistence works. But in many areas the need for action remains. The combination of real and existing problems on the one side and diffuse fears and knee-jerk prejudices on the other are social dynamite, which then explodes in discussions like those outlined above and put a strain on coexistence in school classes, city neighborhoods, or the workplace. It is unnecessary to even mention extreme consequences such as the mass murder carried out by a racist Norwegian fanatic (a Christian, not a Muslim!) in July 2011.

To guard against such developments, to pave the way for successful peaceful coexistence, we need visionary and forward-looking ideas and concepts which do not polarize communities but offer alternatives. The global ethic idea is just such a concept, and the Global Ethic Foundation wants to provide an impetus that will prompt people to rethink and—starting, if possible, with children and adolescents—promote a change of attitude. We want:

- to awaken people's interest in other cultures;

- to communicate knowledge about our own and about foreign cultures and their values;

- to help break down prejudices so that it will be possible to meet in a critical but friendly atmosphere of mutual respect;

- and finally to create an awareness that, despite our
  different areas of life, we can agree on common values
  which will ensure that we can peacefully coexist.

The need for action is evidenced not merely by notorious problem neighborhoods and deprived areas in our big cities. Even in a quiet academic town like Tübingen there are schools with pupils from almost twenty different cultures, ethnic groups, and religions. The precondition for successful coexistence is to know about one another, about differences and similarities, so that prejudices and clichés will not develop. And the foundations for such knowledge about one's own and foreign cultures—such an intercultural and interreligious competence—need to be laid as early as possible, preferably in the family and kindergarten, and the foundation needs to be deepened at school and to be experienced and tested in daily life.

And therefore kindergartens, day-care centers, and above all *schools are primary places in which to learn* about these intercultural questions. From its inception, the Global Ethic Foundation has consistently attempted to make the substance of its work accessible to teachers and—working together with teachers from many different types of schools who teach many different subjects, often after consultation with and support from university educationalists—has developed and field-tested many projects, materials, and instruments for everyday pedagogical use. To describe all of the activities we offer schools in any detail would go far beyond the scope of this publication. Additional information is available on the website of our Foundation at www.weltethos org. A few summarizing comments must suffice:

We were able to gain initial practical experience of working in schools by initiating *classroom competitions*. We began such competitions early on in Germany and Switzerland and later extended them to other countries. We also had a regionally limited competition in Tübingen. The aim of these competitions was to develop course modules and school projects about intercultural coexistence and ethical questions. We received, quite early on, a wide range of very concrete and practical proposals for the pragmatic implementation of these topics in schools and these proposals also demonstrated how exciting, varied, and interesting the discussion of such topics can be for children and adolescents.

- The *multimedia project "Tracing the Way. Spiritual Dimensions of the World Religions,"* which has been mentioned before, is a valuable educational tool. Its seven one-hour films, which will soon also be available in several different languages as an international edition, have become a regular fixture of many media departments and school libraries. The accompanying illustrated volume and interactive CD-ROM are not only used by teachers to prepare for this subject but also in many classrooms.

- Based on this project we created an *exhibition* entitled *World—Universal Peace—Global Ethic.* The exhibition is available in German, English, Italian, and in various formats. It has been successfully used for years not only in Germany but in many countries worldwide. The exhibition has been shown in schools and in various public forums: in banks, town halls, educational establishments and academies, in large organizations such as the headquarters of the United Nations in New York City and the International Monetary Fund in Washington, the halls of religious organizations, the parishes and spiritual centers of the great religions, and in many countries all over the world.

- Our *folder Weltethos in der Schule [Global Ethic in School]*, available thus far only in German, is already in its third edition and numbers some 506 pages. It has met with widespread acceptance. It was developed over many years in close collaboration with teachers and offers a range of teaching materials on our topics for classroom use. An adapted version for use in Swiss schools was developed in collaboration with the Pädagogische Hochschule Zentralschweiz (the Teacher Training College of Central Switzerland).

- Also in cooperation with our Swiss partners, teaching materials for 4 to 8-year-olds have been developed which can be used to make preschool, kindergarten, and elementary school children aware of global ethics topics in an age-appropriate way. They offer a variety of ways to implement ethical principles such as justice, nonviolence, partnership, and truthfulness.

- In the Srihari Global School (Asansol, India) Global Ethic as a separate school subject has been developed and introduced. It is being studied by children from fourth grade through high school graduation. The subject offers not only lessons in the classroom and projects, but also online exchanges with other schools around the world. The teaching materials were modeled on the Swiss materials developed for 4 to 8-year-olds.

- And finally, with our *Internet learning platform "A Global Ethic Now!"* we have moved into a whole new area of media communication. The website allows interested persons to learn about a global ethic interactively and to familiarize themselves with various aspects of the topic (religion, politics, the economy). One area of this learning platform—"Global Ethic in Everyday Life"—has been specifically tailored to the everyday experiences of young people. Using situations that highlight ethical dilemmas that can then be played through interactively, young people can become aware of the fact that they constantly face ethical questions in their everyday lives. The learning platform can be used free of charge and is available in German, English, and French.

- In addition, the Global Ethic Foundation has always offered *courses* and *training sessions for teachers* about the world's religions and many different aspects associated with the topic of a global ethic. We also initiate and offer support for *school projects* and *interreligious initiatives*, providing suggestions on the content of the projects and support to implement them. The *international pedagogical cooperative projects* in Colombia and Hong Kong, which Günther Gebhardt discusses in more detail below, are a particularly welcome development. They show that the ideas, materials, and media we developed are also setting precedents in other countries and cultures, where they are translated and adapted for local use and disseminated across the country.

(3) Learning to live ethical values

There are two key aspects to a global ethic. On the one hand, as described above, the focus is on acquiring knowledge which will allow us to understand people from different cultures and with different life experiences and also understand our own culture better. On the other hand, the focus is on changing awareness, on *communicating values*, on changing attitudes. Both aspects are closely linked; intertwined. An understanding of foreign customs and experiences does not merely require knowledge of experiences and customs but also a willingness to engage with what is foreign and strange. The communication of values cannot occur in the abstract; it always requires knowledge of values and also knowledge of how values are anchored in different cultures and religions, why we need them today for peaceful coexistence, and how people can become more aware of values within their individual circumstances and be motivated to change their attitudes.

Ethical behavior needs to be learned, and it needs to be learned as early as possible. Neurobiologists and educationalists have found that ethical learning does not differ from the way in which we acquire other skills or knowledge in general. Babies are not born as individuals who think and act ethically but as individuals who have the potential to learn how to behave ethically—if they are confronted with ethical behavior. Values such as respect, nonviolence, solidarity, etc. need to be transmitted to children from the day of their birth by persons around them living according to these values. This allows children to acquire this culture of values and to practice them.

Only if children have experienced and learned as early as possible:

- that it is better to assert one's own interests against other people without resorting to aggression and violence;

- that trust will develop only if you do not lie to each other and you know that you can rely on one another;

- that it is better for everyone if you treat each other fairly and even sometimes refrain from pursuing your own advantage;

- that skin color, religion, gender, and personal preferences or handicaps are not a reason for contempt and social marginalization;

- that happy coexistence is only possible if people treat each other humanely;

then, and only then, will these children also behave accordingly later on when they are adolescents or adults. It is not a coincidence that the Global Ethic Declaration of Chicago focused on the values of nonviolence, justice, truthfulness, and partnership and on the principles of Humanity and Reciprocity (Golden Rule).

Such learning and experience of ethical behavior is a process which is most likely to succeed if it starts in the family and continues at school. In general, we refer to this process as education. It is interesting that teaching staff in kindergartens and day-care centers are also referred to as educators in the sense that they bring up children. Teachers in schools, particularly those who teach in senior school, often comment that it is not their job to bring up children; their job is to impart knowledge. Nobody would deny that a central task of teachers is to provide children with sufficient academic qualifications and no school, however outstanding it may be, can make up for neglect in the parental home if children have not been given security and have not been brought up to understand the importance of ethical values. But experienced teachers confirm that as a teacher it is impossible *to not educate* the children. Why? Because the teacher's own personality, the way in which the teacher comes across to children and adolescents, how the teacher listens, responds and reacts to them—in other words, the teacher's personal example—communicates an attitude. This, in turn, will provoke a reaction in the children and adolescents: the teacher will be accepted and can persuade his or her pupils, or the teacher will not be taken seriously or even rejected. This is quite independent of *what* the teacher says—it depends solely on *how* the teacher says it.

Specialist knowledge, methodologies, and didactics by themselves are no guarantee that education will succeed, particularly if it is a question of passing on values. This is why today psychologists and educationalists emphasize the enormous importance of the pattern of interactions in daily school life: the capacity to motivate pupils so that they are prepared to open up and educating them becomes possible at many levels. But this will not occur by itself, it requires a stance with regard to values on the part of the educator, and this in turn requires self-criticism and a measure of self-awareness.

A successful pattern of interaction—in this case between teachers, pupils, and parents—is also essential for the overall *school culture*. Today, many schools have drafted mission statements and codes of behavior in which they state their objectives with regard to peaceful cooperation. Such documents are important and helpful as aids that constantly affirm and reflect these objectives. Every day at school there are challenges that have an ethical dimension: in the relationship between teachers and pupils, in dealing with acts of violence, in the relationship between ethnic groups or between girls and boys, and much more. Of course, schools cannot create values themselves. They need guidelines or programs which can serve as a basis and guide. But such guidelines cannot be left to the imagination of the respective teacher; they need to be compiled as part of a collaborative consensual process that involves all persons shaping the life of the school.

This is an area where the transcultural approach of a global ethic can offer an effective guide, possibly even a concept for a consensus. Teachers can gear their attempts to communicate values to the principles of a global ethic, and these principles will give them a measuring rod that they can use as a guide for their own actions, for the content they teach, and for their teaching methods.

In Germany, many schools have taken this route in the past few years: from a global ethic to a school ethic. It can start with setting up rules for individual classes—rules which are jointly developed and accepted by everyone, and it can expand to include a whole developmental process within the school. In today's multicultural context we need a basic ethical consensus in our schools which derives from and is nourished by many different religions and cultures and which can be placed in the context of the cultures and religions present at the school.

To encourage more schools to support such initiatives, the Global Ethic Foundation awards the designation "Global Ethic School" to recognize schools which do not merely include the global ethic idea in their curriculum but also find ways of incorporating the aims of the global ethic idea and its associated attitudes and values in everyday school life so that everyone involved—pupils, parents, teachers—can experience, test, and live them.

It is important that a school ethic of this type is not limited to declarative statements. The ethic must be tangibly experienced by those involved, it must be continually practiced, and must continually prove its worth in everyday life as a bedrock of values which hold up even in the face of many different challenges and

119

the pressures of school life and which offer an orientation even in situations requiring difficult decisions.

(4) Intercultural and ethical learning in business

In a nutshell, one could say: all that has been said here with regard to the situation in schools and other learning environments applies analogously to business and companies. Or to put it slightly differently: the topics of interculturality and values are equally relevant for companies and also represent a pedagogical challenge, in the widest sense of the word, for business.

This is quite obvious when regarding the interculturality topic. Currently, even small- and medium-sized businesses have to act within a global context; even in rural areas most companies employ people from different cultures. Successful peaceful cooperation requires a minimum of knowledge about one another. This applies, as discussed above, to society in general and it applies in particular also to companies. When more secular cultures collide with more religious cultures, this often leads to irritations and bewilderment. Properly gauging the limits of tolerance on both sides requires sensitivity, openness, and a certain minimum degree of expert knowledge.

Such questions become even more pressing when a company sends their staff to work in foreign cultural areas or the company works together with local companies in distant lands. Consultants generally agree today that this only works if it is done with the necessary intercultural awareness of those involved and is accompanied by good communication of intercultural competences. If business relationships with people from different cultural backgrounds are to be successful, this will require an understanding of behavioral patterns and cultural environments—not to mention the potential for conflicts based on misunderstandings. Such an understanding must go far beyond simply knowing about things such as eating habits, communication patterns, manners, and etiquette. It must include cultural depths; above all, in many cultures an understanding of the foreign culture must include an awareness of the importance of religion in the country, as this can affect people deeply in ways which may often surprise secularized Europeans and will guide people's behavior.

So how do companies deal with such challenges today? Increasing numbers of companies use a professional *human resources management* system which attempts to take account of the cultural diversity of its employees as part of *diversity management*. Many companies are prepared to pay for professional coaching and intercultural training of its employees traveling abroad, particularly if these employees will be staying in foreign countries for longer periods as expatriates. But such topics still appear to be alien to quite a few companies, particularly medium-sized businesses. They bank on their employees somehow managing to get on with one another and will, at best, only intervene to keep the peace within the company if culturally or religiously motivated conflicts threaten. And as far as preparing their staff members when they go abroad, very often this is limited to offering organizational support; even larger companies often only offer their future representatives abroad an intercultural crash course in a few hours, which at best communicates the sort of knowledge available from guidebooks—a far cry, at all events, from teaching them any deeper understanding of a foreign culture. Then it comes as a surprise when the employees working abroad fail because even after several years, they simply do not understand their local colleagues and business partners.

What of the *ethical* dimension? Of course, a company requires structures, institutions, guidelines, and strategies that give due consideration to ethical questions in today's complex world of business. Much of this has already been touched on in the chapter "Economics and a Global Ethic." But in the end, it depends on people and on whether people can be won over. Ultimately it depends on people, on their decisions and personal actions, whether ethical principles will be reflected in day-to-day business. In the end, it is a question of the attitude of the individual which will determine whether an ethical company culture will prevail or fail. And such attitudes must be learned; individuals must reflect on them and practice them so that they can maintain them in the big and small decisions of their professional life and, perhaps, even inspire others. It was no coincidence that a high-ranking participant in another seminar for business leaders commented that with regard to ethical questions she often achieved more through a good discussion than by sending out reams of paper and setting up complicated processes.

And therefore the Global Ethic Foundation focuses also on a global economic ethic as its first core issue in its Global Ethic Institute at the University of Tübingen.

(5) A Global Ethic Institute

Interestingly, the impetus to set up such an institute came from industry, to be more precise, from the south German industrialist Karl Schlecht. The question of ethics in business and in companies had long been a central issue for Karl Schlecht. Inspired by the topic of a global ethic, he has supported the work of the Global Ethic Foundation together with his wife Brigitte for many years. He funded the Global Ethic Institute which was set up in May 2011 and commenced operations in the summer semester of 2012.

Further information on the institute is available on the website of our foundation.

To make a long story short, the purpose and the task of the Global Ethic Institute is to anchor the extensive agenda of the Global Ethic Foundation in the university's research and teaching and to continue to support work in this field, the scope of which has been amply demonstrated in this book.

In addition to their research work, the scholars working at the institute will develop innovative teaching courses for the University of Tübingen: seminars and lecture series, courses for academics, and lecture series for the general public.

One of the institute's core areas will be to outline the basis for a global economic ethic and place it in a concrete framework. A global economic ethic professorship has been established at the institute. There are also places available for national and international scholars and teachers to research and teach at the institute for limited periods of time which ensures that it can offer a wide range of courses on numerous different topics.

In addition to basic research and teaching on questions of a global economic ethic, the Global Ethic Institute develops and propagates useful concepts for the practical implementation of a global economic ethic. The goal is to make students—who will one day be the decision makers in companies, industry, and society—more aware of ethical questions and to offer them a practical preparation for their subsequent working life.

For further information see:
http://www.weltethos-institut.org.

4. The foundation: a worldwide global ethic (Günther Gebhardt)

(1) How the Global Ethic Foundation developed

It was like a fairy story! The name of the fairytale prince was Count Karl Konrad von der Groeben (1918-2005) who one day in 1995 rang Professor Hans Küng. Professor Küng was shortly going to retire from his university work. Count Groeben had been inspired by reading the book *Global Responsibility*. He believed that putting these ideas into practice in society was precisely what was required in these times which appeared to offer so little in terms of ethical orientation. Count Groeben, a former industrialist, had sold his companies in his old age and was looking to find a meaningful use for his fortune. He was prepared, he said, to provide enough capital to set up a foundation headed by Hans Küng which would devote itself to disseminating the idea of a global ethic.

This fabulous offer came at exactly the right time. Once he had become professor emeritus in 1996, Hans Küng would no longer have been able to make use of the university's infrastructure for his work and it is doubtful whether it would have been possible to continue working on the global ethic project. But now Count Groeben set up the Global Ethic Foundation for Intercultural and Inter-religious Research, Education and Encounters with an endowment of five million German marks and thus made it possible for Hans Küng and his team to continue their work without interruption. The foundation was officially established with an opening ceremony held at the University of Tübingen on October 23, 1995. The inauguration lecture was given by the Prime Minister of the German Federal State of Baden-Württemberg, Erwin Teufel, who as a member of the foundation's board of trustees still maintains close ties to the foundation. Hans Küng as the president of the foundation spoke on the topic of "Global Ethic and Education." This was a topic that had long been close to the heart of the foundation's benefactor. Right from the start, Count Groeben and his wife Ria had wanted the new foundation to focus on communicating the global ethic idea to children and disseminating the idea in schools. This was the mandate and the Global Ethic Foundation has been putting it into practice over the years on an increasingly professional scale.

Not long after the foundation was established in Germany, a global ethic foundation was also set up in 1996 in Hans Küng's native country of Switzerland. Martita Jöhr-Rohr (1912-2008), a philanthropist from Zurich, had been similarly inspired by the idea of a global ethic and donated part of her own fortune and that of her deceased husband Adolf Jöhr—formerly professor for economics in St. Gall—to set up the Global Ethic Foundation Switzerland with an office in Zurich. Until 2013, Hans Küng was also the president of this foundation.

Over the years official global ethic foundations or similar associations came into existence in Austria, the Czech Republic, Slovenia, Columbia, Mexico, and Brazil. For local reasons, activities in the Czech Republic and Brazil have ceased for now. But the foundation has contacts and partners in many more countries. All of them will be briefly mentioned below. It is, of course, impossible to provide a complete report of the foundation's global work. Information on this can be obtained on the foundation's website: www.global-ethic.org. These few pages will only offer an overview and some particularly important recent examples.

It should become clear: a global ethic is not a mere scholarly idea but a project which attempts to find ways to promote ethical consciousness, open and fair dialogue between people, and intercultural competence at many levels in practice. The impact of this project now extends far beyond the groves of academia into many different areas of public life, politics, business, the sciences, schools, and general education, every area which requires that people respect "the rules of the game," into areas both big and small, where people with different religions and from different cultures meet to learn from one another and to discover, despite all their differences, the many things they have in common, particularly in the matter of ethics.

(2) The foundation promotes education

For the idea of a global ethic to put down roots in people and societies, comprehensive and correct knowledge of other cultures and religions is necessary, together with a sensitivity regarding the relevance of ethical questions in an intercultural context. This can be cultivated through teaching and education. Numerous different educational events have taken place over the years— hundreds of lectures, seminars, and conferences. They include national and international events, religious and nonreligious events, and events where the many dimensions and facets of the global ethic idea have been presented and made accessible to the general public or specialist audiences. In European countries this teaching is to some extent carried out by the staff of the Tübingen Foundation but also to a great extent by an increasing number of highly capable independent speakers, many of whom have a background in education. It would exceed the scope of this contribution to list all the speakers and contributors here, particularly as the group is continually changing. Interested persons can refer to the comprehensive and constantly updated German website of our foundation: www.weltethos.org. The website also gives the dates of public lectures by speakers of the foundation worldwide.

Audiovisual media can be particularly effective in education. Since the 1990s the foundation has therefore developed a number of educational packages and materials using different media, as described by Stephan Schlensog in the previous article:

- The multimedia project "Tracing the Way: Spiritual Dimensions of the World Religions:" consists of seven television films in which Hans Küng presents seven religions and explores original locations: the indigenous religions of Australia and Africa, Hinduism, Chinese religion, Buddhism, Judaism, Christianity, and Islam. An illustrated textbook to accompany the film series and an interactive CD-ROM are also available.

- The exhibition "World Religions—Universal Peace— Global Ethic" consists of fifteen panels which present the basic elements of the ethical teachings of eight world religions and the seven principles and directives of a global ethic. Available in German, English, and Italian and in various formats (also as posters particularly for use in schools), since its inception the exhibition has been showcased many times in Germany and abroad.

- The folder "Weltethos in der Schule" ["Global Ethic in School"]: consists of 500 worksheets and texts for use in schools together with instructions for teachers. All of these materials were compiled by teachers and tested in schools. They have aroused much interest in other countries as well, including India and China.

- The most innovative teaching medium is, without a doubt, the online global ethic learning platform entitled "A Global Ethic Now!" available in German, English, and French. Interested persons all over the world can work through different aspects of a global ethic with the help of numerous pictures, texts, and sound recordings.

Sensitivity with regard to ethical behavior and respect for other people and for a global ethic needs to be imparted early to children and adolescents. Therefore, right from the foundation's inception, work in schools was always considered particularly important. The article by Stephan Schlensog offers more detail on this point.

(3) The foundation is internationally active

Right from the start, the Global Ethic Foundation had numerous contacts and collaborated with partners in many different countries and continents. This was only natural, as the charter of the global ethic ideas, the Declaration Toward a Global Ethic, was developed by Hans Küng together with an international group of advisers and subsequently adopted by an international gathering, the 1993 Parliament of the World's Religions in Chicago. Numerous basic works on a global ethic have been translated into the major languages and into many smaller ones. The intercultural and interreligious aspect is a core element of the global ethic project and requires that activities be international. The interest in the global ethic idea in different areas of the world has increased over the years and has resulted in some extraordinary projects. The international lectures given by Hans Küng and other members of the foundation's staff often played an important role in providing a stimulus.

China

In 1979, only three years after the death of Mao Zedong, Hans Küng was able to give a talk at the Chinese Academy for the Social Sciences in Beijing on the question of whether God exists. The foundation was able to build on these contacts: in 1997 and in 2001 scholarly conferences were held in Beijing, which examined the relevance of a global ethic for China and noted the convergence between a global ethic and traditional Chinese ethics (Confucius). At the Second International Conference on Sinology at Renmin University in Beijing the 2009 inaugural address was given by Hans Küng. Stephan Schlensog has also given talks in Beijing, Hong Kong, and Shanghai. In September 2010 the noted philosopher Professor Tu Weiming set up an Institute for Advanced Humanistic Studies at Peking University (Beida) with a Centre for World Religions and a Global Ethic.

The activities of the Global Ethic Foundation in China found expression also at a practical and pedagogical level, especially in Hong Kong. Together with the supervisory school authorities and the Hong Kong Institute of Education, the foundation's partners in the (Protestant) Institute of Sino-Christian Studies in Hong Kong carried out a major educational project from 2008 to 2016 with the aim of introducing the Global Ethic into the Hong Kong school system. Forty teaching projects have been developed using teaching materials from the Global Ethic Foundation, and several textbooks and teacher's manuals on ethical topics have been published. There is an exhibition that uses comics to give pupils an understanding of the world religions and the global ethic concept. The materials are available to all schools and teachers in Hong

Kong on the website of the state education authority. An interfaith council with representatives of Buddhism, Christianity, Islam, Confucianism, and Taoism is monitoring the project.

Other Asian Countries

In *Malaysia* in 2005, Peter Schier, the representative of the Konrad Adenauer Foundation (KAS) at the time, had the exhibition "World Religions—Universal Peace—Global Ethic" translated into the local language Bahasa and into Chinese and exhibited the translations with great success in Kuala Lumpur and Penang. Here again, the focus of attention was on pedagogical aspects, and there were numerous intensive interreligious encounters linked to the exhibition. At one of the conferences in Kuala Lumpur organized by the KAS in December 2005, representatives from the Ministry of Education and from school authorities from eleven Southeast Asian countries discussed the application of a global ethic in schools. The opening lectures at the conference were given by Hans Küng and Günther Gebhardt.

As an international speaker of the Global Ethic Foundation, Peter Schier also gave introductory lectures on the global ethic idea in 2009 and 2010 at intercultural conferences in Bangladesh and India, later also in Cambodia. There had already been an academic conference in Delhi in 1997 on the relationship between a global ethic and Indian ethics.

In India, a project to spread the global ethic idea in schools was started in cooperation with the Indian SREI Foundation and supported by the Robert Bosch Foundation. As part of this project, global ethic study materials for children aged 4 to 8 years were translated and adapted to Indian requirements. The pilot school chosen for the project was the Srihari Global School in Asansol, and the global ethic was introduced as a separate school subject. For details, see the previous article by Stephan Schlensog.

Middle East

At a time where Muslims are increasingly mistrusted and there are large-scale upheavals in the Middle East, the promotion of a dialogue between Jews, Christians, and Muslims and a recollection of what these religions have in common at an ethical level is particularly close to the heart of the Global Ethic Foundation. Prior to the development of the global ethic project, lecture tours by Hans Küng in the Middle East had already created a basis of mutual trust. Particularly important in this context were a number of lectures held in Israel and early scholarly contacts in Iran (for example to Mohammad Khatami, later to become a reformist president of Iran) and to persons interested in interreligious dialogue such as Prince Hassan of Jordan, later also to government circles in the Sultanate of Oman which supported religious policies of tolerance and dialogue.

In 2007 — it was as yet impossible to presage the upheavals which would occur four years later — Professor Küng undertook an important lecture tour to Cairo and Damascus which also touched on religious policies. Particularly important for the dissemination of the global ethic idea in Arabic countries was a lecture and a high-level conference held at the American University in Cairo. The Goethe Institute (German Cultural Institute) in Damascus and the Syrian publishing company Dar al-Fikr invited Professor Küng to give a talk in Damascus in front of religious leaders, students, and the general public. The book *Global Responsibility* was translated into Arabic in 1998 in Lebanon, and a number of translations of theological works and works on a global ethic have come out in recent years in Iran, together with an Arabic version of the book *Why Do We Need a Global Ethic?* which was translated and provided with an extensive commentary for Arabic readers by Thabet Eid (Zurich). He also published an Arabic translation of large parts of Hans Küng's book *Islam* with extensive comments. A freelance lecturer of the Global Ethic Foundation, the Muslim scholar Muhammad Sameer Murtaza has been doing important educational work for the global ethic project, particularly among Muslim audiences in Germany.

South America

The development of the global ethic project is always good for a few surprises. Contacts to countries in South America were not a major priority for the foundation when in 2006, almost at the same time, three personages from Columbia, Mexico, and Brazil approached the Global Ethic Foundation and formulated their interest in global ethic activities and the setting up of global ethic foundations in their own countries. For Columbia this was Carlos Paz, a lawyer and well-known promoter of projects, for Mexico the entrepreneur and philanthropist Gerardo Martinez Cristerna, and for Brazil the professor of German studies Paulo Soethe (Curitiba), who provided important contacts to the University UNISINOS in Sao Leopoldo, in particular to the Instituto Humanitas headed by Inacio Neutzling. These partners of the Global Ethic Foundation in Brazil, Columbia, and Mexico energetically and efficiently organized a series of lecture tours in 2007 in their respective countries for Hans Küng (who was accompanied on some of them by Stephan Schlensog), and with surprising speed they set up their own global ethic foundations (Columbia and Mexico) or established a global ethic office (Brazil). Sadly, the Global Ethic Office in Brazil was later forced to cease its work for internal reasons. In all of these countries, the global ethic idea has been welcomed with an encouraging display of interest by business, in politics, in academic circles, and by representatives from many different areas of society.

There are many interesting and creative projects which have been launched in these countries since 2006. But the most spectacular one certainly deserves a mention: Carlos Paz, the director of Columbia's global ethic foundation (Fundación Ética Mundial) successfully kicked off an enormous project to disseminate the global ethic idea in the media. From November 2009 to July 2010 Columbia's biggest daily newspaper El Tiempo once a week included a small booklet on individual aspects of the global ethic idea. In addition, a comprehensive textbook on a global ethic was compiled in collaboration with El Tiempo which examined numerous ethically relevant topics using a global ethic as its starting point, and presented them in many different creative ways. In the years that followed, Carlos Paz also set up working groups with entrepreneurs to consider ethics in an economic context and published handbooks on environmental ethics and political ethics for citizens. A slim anthology of the lectures Hans Küng held in South America ("Ética mundial en América Latina") published in 2008 by the publishing company Trotta (Madrid) also helps disseminate the idea of a global ethic throughout this continent.

Switzerland

The Stiftung Weltethos Schweiz is the oldest subsidiary of the Tübingen Global Ethic Foundation. The establishment of this Swiss foundation in 1996 was already described above. From the start, the Swiss foundation's activities focused on work in schools and on showcasing the exhibition "World Religions— Universal Peace—Global Ethic" which, together with the accompanying brochure, had also been produced and issued by the Swiss foundation in French. It was possible to show the exhibition in numerous locations, big and small, within Switzerland over a period of several years, often accompanied by talks or other global ethic events.

As in Germany, the foundation in Switzerland has set itself the important pedagogical task of communicating the global ethic idea in schools. The Swiss foundation organized competitions in schools both in the German-speaking and French-speaking parts of Switzerland. School classes were encouraged to develop teaching modules on topics associated with a global ethic and the world's religions, and the best ones were awarded prizes by the foundation. The Swiss foundation's involvement in pedagogical activities in Switzerland culminated in an official cooperation agreement, concluded in 2009, with the Department for Ethics, Religions and Culture of the Teacher Training College of Central Switzerland (PHZ) in Goldau. Up until 2011, nine different projects were carried out, ranging from a project competition for school classes to training courses and the development of teaching materials on a global ethic. Since 2018, the Swiss Global Ethic Foundation has been working together with the St. Gallen University of Teacher Education on a national educational project to create teaching units for primary schools on "Ethics–Religion–Community" for use in schools all over Switzerland.

Austria

The Austrian Initiative for a Global Ethic (IWEO), domiciled in Vienna, is not a foundation but a society (legally established in 2005) and had been active already several years before. As is often the case, it owes its existence largely to the involvement of a single person and her enthusiasm for the idea of a global ethic: Professor Edith Riether. With her untiring work as the initiative's long-time general secretary since 2000 and as its president since 2010, she has been able to bring in a number of key persons from different areas of society and different religions to become members of the society and the society's steering committee. Over the years she has initiated and implemented numerous activities. Annual lecture series at universities in Vienna have been held since 2005; the lectures often focus on the more unusual aspects of a global ethic such as technology, animal ethics, or psychology, and have enjoyed extensive coverage, helped by a number of anthologies published to accompany the series.

Education and schools have also played an important role in Austria. The IWEO champions the introduction of ethics classes in schools based on the global ethic project. The IWEO organized a poster competition on the Golden Rule and an essay competition on the principles of a global ethic. With seminars for teachers, general lectures, and the exhibition "World Religions—Universal Peace—Global Ethic," Edith Riether and others are helping to make the idea of a global ethic better known in Austria.

The "Innsbruck Forum for the Academic Promotion of the Global Ethic Project" under the leadership of Professor Emeritus Helmut Reinalter works independently of the IWEO. The primary task of this forum is a scholarly reflection on the different dimensions of a global ethic in symposiums, lecture series, and publications.

Czech Republic

In 2000 the lecturer and retired senator Dr. Karel Floss set up a Czech Global Ethic Foundation. Karel Floss focused on promoting the idea of a global ethic, particularly in political circles, and on supporting work on the philosophical analysis of the global ethic idea in symposiums and publications. The translation of a number of books by Hans Küng on a global ethic into Czech also owes much to his initiative. But the Czech Global Ethic Foundation is currently not carrying out any activities.

Slovenia

The Slovenian Global Ethic Initiative mainly organizes public lectures and seminars on social and ethically relevant topics and features regularly in the media. The publication of the Slovenian translation of this *Global Ethic Handbook*, which was supported by the Global Ethic Initiative, has been particularly important for spreading the global ethic idea in Slovenia.

In addition to these official European partner foundations and initiatives, a number of groups and institutions exist in various other countries which also work toward promoting the idea of a global ethic, for example through translating and disseminating publications and materials of the Global Ethic Foundation, by showing the exhibition, by hosting conferences, holding educational events, or carrying out projects in schools. This has been the case, for example, in Bosnia-Herzegovina, Croatia, Italy, France, and Luxembourg.

United Nations

What was highly gratifying and almost completely unexpected was the impact of the global ethic idea in the United Nations. After Hans Küng had given a talk in 1992 and again in 1999 in the headquarters of the United Nations in New York, he contributed in 2001, as previously mentioned, to a manifesto commissioned by the then UN General Secretary Kofi Annan on the dialogue between cultures which aimed to develop conclusive guidelines for international politics at the dawn of the 21st century. These were later published as *Crossing the Divide*. The idea of a global ethic also cropped up in many passages of this valuable and groundbreaking document. The exhibition "World Religions—Universal Peace—Global Ethic" was even shown in 2001, directly after the devastating terrorist attacks in New York and Washington, in the UN building in New York, and one year later in the building of the International Monetary Fund (IMF) in Washington, where it was opened by the then managing director of the IMF, Dr. Horst Köhler, together with Hans Küng.

It was, therefore, no coincidence that Kofi Annan held the much-praised Third Global Ethic Lecture in December 2003 in Tübingen: a convincing and unambiguous plea in support of common universal values and the necessity to stand up for them in the teeth of all opposition. The annual global ethic lectures are a kind of shop window for the Global Ethic Foundation with a huge public impact and extensive media coverage.

(4) Academic research, publications, and events remain important for the foundation

The many different activities of the Global Ethic Foundation described in this chapter would not have been possible without a sound scholarly body of research compiled by Hans Küng and others over many decades. An overview of the basic literature which originated over the years is available from the Foundation's website, while the most important publications on the topic of a global ethic are listed at the end of this book. It is not only the foundation which has continued to move in new directions; a broad interdisciplinary discourse has been launched, both at a national and international level, on the topic of a global ethic. The foundation has held academic symposiums, for example in China and India, on the specific contribution of these cultures to an ethic for all of humanity. But there have also been a number of interdisciplinary conferences, the most important of which are briefly listed below:

- "Globale Unternehmen–globales Ethos" [Global Companies – Global Ethic], Baden-Baden 2001 (with managers from several big international corporations, economists and ethicists);

- "Ein neues Paradigma der internationalen Beziehungen" [A new paradigm for international relationships], Tübingen 2002 (with peace researchers, political scientists, and historians);

- "Genese der Moral" [The genesis of morality], Tübingen 2006 (with theologians, philosophers, and developmental biologists);

- "Science and Religion," Tübingen 2006 (with theologians and specialists from many different areas of science, from prehistory to astrophysics);

- "Weltreligionen als Faktoren der Weltpolitik" [World religions as factors for world politics], Tübingen 2007 (with scholars from different religions and members of the InterAction Council of Former Heads of State and Government);

- "Manifest Globales Wirtschaftsethos" [Manifesto for a global economic ethic], New York and Basle 2009 (with industrialists, economists, and ethicists);

- "Global Ethic, Law and Policy," Georgetown University Washington 2011 (with experts in international law, other legal scholars, political scientists, and ethicists).

For the Global Ethic Foundation, the creation of a Global Ethic Institute at the University of Tübingen in 2011 has opened up completely new prospects with regard to practical and academic work on the global ethic project. For more information please refer to the comments by Stephan Schlensog in this volume.

The translation of the global ethic idea into music, which will be discussed by Hans Küng below, was a particular challenge.

5. Translation into music

Personal background: From the beginning, the Global Ethic Foundation has not focused on interreligious dialogue alone but also on other issues, for example in the areas of education and schools, politics and business, even a global ethic in world sports. What was lacking up to now was the transposition of the topic into the arts. A global ethic should not appeal to the head alone; it also needs to appeal to the heart and the emotions. Music, as the most spiritual of the arts, is peculiarly suited to do this.

For many years I had been considering the question of how a global ethic could be represented in musical form. I myself am neither a musician nor a musicologist, but I am a lover of music and since my youth a keen listener of music, who starts every day with music and who often lets himself be transported and delighted by music throughout the day. I have devoted lectures and essays to three of the great masters, Mozart, Wagner, Bruckner; the essays were published in the book "Musik und Religion" [Music and Religion] (Munich 2006).

The work involved was at least an indirect preparation for the global ethic music project.

(1) What the composition WELTETHOS is about

After all this preliminary spadework the question suggested itself: Could the idea of a global ethic be combined directly with music? How could ethical standards be expressed in music or even as an entire musical composition? Such a composition would need to make listeners conscious of humanity's common ethical heritage and reveal how this common heritage can be found in the traditions of the great religions and philosophies and how today it can be and is shared by both believers and nonbelievers. As I started to reflect on the project of such a composition, it quickly became clear that the starting point would be the setting of original texts from the most important religious and philosophical traditions to music, texts which bear witness to an already existing ethic for humanity, as is manifested in transcultural ethical values, standards, and attitudes. And so I penned a master plan for the six movements, with an introductory recitative by a speaker and a refrain concluding every movement to be sung by a children's choir. All in all,, it would be an attempt at creating a tonal vision that embodied a global shift in attitudes.

What sort of concept would be required with regard to the content? My idea was to combine one of the six principles or basic values of a global ethic—humanity, reciprocity, nonviolence, justice, truthfulness, partnership—with one of the six great religious traditions of humanity: with Chinese, Hindu, Buddhist, Jewish, Christian, and Muslim traditions. But these basic values would, of course, not be ascribed exclusively to a single religion, but instead expressed affirmatively as a particular characteristic in the form of a key quotation from the specific tradition and by a recitative which would lead up to it.

(2) *Realization of the concept*

I developed this concept but then I had the greatest trouble in finding a proficient composer for this exquisitely difficult work which would include a big orchestra, a choir, and a children's choir. I was not able to find someone in the German-speaking countries but success finally beckoned in Great Britain in the person of the well-known composer Jonathan Harvey who demonstrated outstanding knowledge of and sensitivity for the music of ancient civilizations. For Harvey, the ethical texts represented something entirely new and different from what he had previously set to music: "These are pragmatic, noble, and ethical texts rather than poetical or mystical; their purpose is more social than aesthetic." The musical translation of the global ethic idea represented an enormous artistic challenge.

My attention had been drawn to Harvey by the Berlin Philharmonic, its artistic director at the time Pamela Rosenberg, and its principal conductor Sir Simon Rattle. Financially, this big commission to compose music in the service of an understanding among nations was made possible by the Swiss Agency for Development and Cooperation (SDC) under Walter Fust, its director at the time. The world premiere of the great work WELTETHOS finally took place on October 13, 2011 (the second performance was on October 15) and was performed by the Berlin Philharmonic conducted by Sir Simon Rattle, the Berlin Radio Choir under Simon Halsey, and the children's choirs of the Georg-Friedrich-Händel Senior School. It will be performed in English by the City of Birmingham Symphony Orchestra conducted by Edward Gardner on June 21, 2012, in Birmingham at the opening of the Cultural Olympiad, and in the Royal Festival Hall in London on October 7. At the suggestion of some English experts the German title WELTETHOS was retained (similar to "Weltanschauung" or "Weltschmerz") for the English score.

(3) Not a mix of religions but peaceful diversity

It was important that the six movements were not written by six different composers to avoid the stringing together of six very different compositions. But a global ethic does not want to mix the externalities of religions together to form a single unified religion—its goal is peace between the religions and individual nations. That was why it was important to avoid creating a musical medley which would merely consist of a colorful succession of melodies and styles which did not originally belong together, adorned with bridging passages of music. The aim was to create an integrated work cast from the same mold, but one which would not exclude the use of modern options such as transposition, defamiliarization, and polyphonic layering.

Many postmodern religious medleys are difficult to bear, and they cannot generally be theologically justified. Every individual can mix together their own spiritual or theological cocktail until it agrees with their personal preferences and needs, limited in many cases to the comfortable aspects of religion. But the emergence of a long-awaited, single unified religion for all people is an unrealistic illusion. What is conceivable and has in many places already been implemented at a local level is a single Christian church, because such a community already has Jesus Christ as the core belief of its faith. However, because of the striving for power and the blindness of various hierarchies, this unity is only rarely apparent. The great religions of the world do not have such a shared fundamental belief. They differ with regard to their origins and their history and have often competed against each other or waged war on one another. To simply presume that they share a common mysticism will only work as long as one keeps quiet and does not talk about what this type of mystical unity could be.

The goal today cannot be a single uniform religion. Rather than wishing for a unity of religions we should strive for peace between the religions and thus also for peace between nations. But peace is never simply a matter for the head and the intellect; it is also a matter for the heart and the emotions. And what could speak more clearly to the heart than music which understands and speaks the language of the heart?

Thus, with this composition, a daring attempt was made to create a musical dialogue and a relationship between the great religious traditions. Admittedly, such an attempt would be doomed to failure from the outset if one were to attempt to base it on common articles of faith. The founding figures of the religions are too different, their religious convictions, theologies, and dogma too varied. But despite all this, they do have something crucial in common—this is impressively demonstrated in the original texts of the different traditions—in their instructions and command-ments, in their practical behavior, in their morality, and in their ethic. This shared common ground as regards the core constitu-ents of their ethics needs to find its musical expression. It is a message which aims for more humanity.

(4) *Libretto of the WELTETHOS composition*

Movement I: Humanity

SPEAKER (on CONFUCIUS)
There was a man in China,
born and died in Qufu/Shandong,
two thousand five hundred years past yet known today.
Unsettled were the times, wars and rebellions frequent.

'Master' he was called,
and was no guru or prophet.
He was a *teacher of wisdom*, the master whose name was 'Kong.'
But the powerful rejected his counsel.
Minister just for a year, yet he had pupils,
and they preserved his teaching.

Heaven he respected, the timeless order.
Studied the old and their customs.
Poetry he loved and also music.
But human beings were his concern, and humanity.

CHOIR (whisper):
The powerful rejected his counsel.
Yet he had pupils who preserved his teachings.
Heaven he respected, its eternal order.
Poetry he loved and also music.
But humankind was his concern and humankind's humanity.

CHOIR:
The Master spoke:
At fifteen I was resolved to learn decisively,
at thirty stood firm,

at forty I was free from doubts,
at fifty I recognized the will of heaven,
at sixty was I even more eager to learn,
at seventy could I follow wishes of my heart
without offending and violating what is right.
 (Confucius, Sayings 2, 4)

CHOIR:
A man without humanity,
what use to him are the rituals?
A woman without humanity,
what use to her is music?
(Confucius, Sayings 3, 3)

REFRAIN (CHILDREN'S CHOIR):
We have a future:
We children have a future, if we're always *human creatures.*
Humans with our minds and hearts.
If young or old, rich or poor, white or colored, man or woman:
Every being shall act with humanity!
Let us humans be humane!

Live! Live! Live in humanity!
We boys have a future.
We girls have a future.
We children have a future, if we're always human,
humans with our minds and hearts.
Let us humans human be!

Movement II: Golden Rule

SPEAKER (on MOSES):
He was chosen long past in Egypt,
to speak for God and lead the people,
the model prophet.
Through the desert he led, there he received God's Torah,
with its humane commandments:
'Do not murder, do not lie, do not steal, do not commit adultery.'
A great legacy to humankind.

The voices of Israel's prophets still warn,
'Be just, be truthful, be loyal, show peace.'
For great and humble the law's teachers interpret them.

Early on the rule was found,
it was framed in distant China,
Golden is still its name.

CHOIR (whisper):
Through the desert he led,
and God's Torah was given to him,
Humanity's commandments.
The voices of Israel's prophets
demand truth, constancy, and peace.

CHOIR:
(Golden Rule)
Do not do to others,
what you don't want
done to you.
(Rabbi Hillel, Sabbath 31a)

CHOIR:
As a compatriot in your very own country
you shall value the stranger, who lives with you,
and you shall him cherish as yourself.
 (Leviticus 19:34)

REFRAIN (CHILDREN'S CHOIR):
We have a future:
We children have a future, if we're always human creatures.
Humans with our minds and hearts.
No racism, no sexism, no nationalism!
We don't want to be egotistical,
we are responsible for each other.

Live! Live! Live in peace!
We boys have a future.
We girls have a future.
We children have a future, if we're always human,
humans with our minds and hearts.
Let us humans human be!

Movement III: Nonviolence

SPEAKER (on INDIA'S GODS):
Countless the gods. Countless the gurus,
Countless India's myths, rites, and legends,
witnessing divine actions
in the all-embracing cosmic order.

Deep within human souls
the wise sought the world's foundation:
the first beginnings of all that is,
source of the universe, world and gods.

Among them is Shiva, highly revered,
the cosmic creator dancer,
and Vishnu, showing himself ever anew in human form.
As Krishna he points the way to final redemption,
grounded in knowledge, love, and a virtuous life.

Bridling the senses, controlling the self
leads human beings to happiness.
Only those who when acting heed all things living,
become free and so attain their highest goal.

CHOIR:
Kindness, Truthfulness.
Not angry, renunciation, not telling tales,
compassion with existence.
Creator, cosmic dancer,
Vishnu, always revealing himself anew.
Truthfulness, not telling tales.
Union with existence,
nonattachment, mildness, shamefulness,
strongly steadfast.
Become a part of someone who is born for a divine destiny...
the destiny divine leads to redemption.
(Mahabharata VI, 40, 2-5)

CHOIR:
Nonviolence, truthfulness, not stealing,
Creator, cosmic dancer,
pure way of life without craving for possessions
is the ultimate discipline.
(Patañjali, Yogasutra II, 30)

Krishna shows the way to ultimate liberation,
Nonviolence, wisdom, knowledge.
(Law of Manu VI, 92)

REFRAIN (CHILDREN'S CHOIR):
We have a future:
We children have a future,
if we're always human creatures.
Humans with our minds and hearts.
No, not hate and spite, not violence and criminality.
Let us humans be humane!

Live! Live! Live in freedom!
We boys have a future.
We girls have a future.
We children have a future, if we're always human,
humans with our minds and hearts.
Let us humans human be!

CHOIR:
No brother should his brother despise,
no sister her sister
speak your words in harmony,
with the same goal at one, in friendliness.
(Atharva Veda 3, 30)

Movement IV: Justice

SPEAKER (on MUHAMMAD):
The way, the truth and the life,
the Prophet and statesman of Islam was and is not,
That was and is God's revelation, the holy book.
'Submit to the one and only God,

149

the just and merciful,' that is its call.
And an ethic of justice:
'Do not be selfish or seek earthly goods,
show solidarity with all.'
This is the Prophet's message.

CHOIR (a cappella):
Hast thou ere considered who gives the lie to the final
Judgement?
It is he, one who throws out the orphan and feels no urge to ask
the needy to table.
Woe to the praying ones, woe to those whose hearts are far from
prayer,
those who want only to be looked at and be praised for acts of
charity.
(Qur'an, Surah 107:1-7)

CHOIR:
None of you is a believer,
so long as he does not for his brother wish
what he wishes for himself.
(40 Hadithe von an-Nawawi 13)

And be good to your neighbor,
thus will you a believer be.
And wish for everyone
that which you for yourself wish ...
(at-Tirmidhi, Hadith 2305)

REFRAIN (CHILDREN'S CHOIR):
We have a future:
We children have a future,
if we're always human creatures.

Humans with our minds and hearts.
No, not hunger and poverty,
not greed and corruption.
Let us humans be humane!
Live! Live! Live! in Justice!
We boys have a future.
We girls have a future.
We children have a future, if we're always human,
humans with our minds and hearts.
Let us humans human be!

Movement V: Truth

SPEAKER (on BUDDHA GAUTAMA):
Son of a prince was he;
he had it all: wife, child, and riches.
Yet faced with the pain of the world,
with old age, sickness, and death,
he gave everything up, becoming a beggar monk.
Yet not through hard austerities,
but by meditation and deep immersion
he found what he long desired: illumination, liberation.
He saw through suffering and what brings sorrow:
hatred, blindness, and greed.
As a way to salvation abandoning self-cherishing
to become free for compassion with all living creatures.
An eightfold path away from the self:
right recognition and right views—knowledge,
right speech, right action, right life—ethic,
right effort, attentiveness, and recollection—illumination.

CHOIR:
May you not be misled by rumor, by tradition
do not be led by hearsay.
May you neither be misled by the proof of religious texts'
authority,
or by its pure logic, or by its logical inclusions,
or by respect for externalities, or by a delight in speculative
opinions,
or by seeming appearances, by the idea this is your master.
But if you in yourself know that certain things are unhealthy, false
and evil,
then give them up.
And if you in yourself know that certain things are healthy and
good
then take them up and follow them.
(Vimamsaka Sutta)

CHOIR:
Rightful knowledge, rightful perspectives,
rightful wisdom, rightful compassion,
rightful speaking, rightful action,
rightful living, rightful effort,
rightful attention, rightful concentration.

REFRAIN (CHILDREN'S CHOIR):
We have a future:
We children have a future,
if we're always human creatures.
Humans with our minds and hearts.
No, not lying and deception,
not hypocrisy and demagogy.
Let us humans be humane!
Live! Live! Live! in truthfulness!

We boys have a future.
We girls have a future.
We children have a future, if we're always human,
humans with our minds and hearts.
Let us humans human be!

Movement VI: Partnership

SPEAKER (on JESUS OF NAZARETH):
A man aged thirty,
hidden in a corner of Rome's great empire made history.
Travelling round Israel he preached,
nearer to God than the priests,
freer from the world than the ascetics,
more moral far than the moralists,
more revolutionary than any revolution.
God's kingdom, God's will he proclaims,
aimed at human well-being;
he argued for a love which includes the enemy,
serves without hierarchy,
denies itself, not seeking reward,
in endless forgiveness,
shows solidarity with the poor,
the blessed of this world.
He paid with his life in a cruel death.
But for believers he lives in God's eternity.
Love, his message, abides.

CHOIR:

"Though I speak with tongues of angels and men
but love have not,
So am I a sounding brass or a clangorous cymbal.
And though I possessed prophets' powers,
and understood all mysteries,
and had all knowledge.
And though I had all faith so that I could remove mighty
mountains
but love have not, so would I be nothing.
Though I gave away all my possessions,
and gave my body to burn,
but love had not, to me it profits nothing.
Love is fortitudinous and friendly.
Love has no jealousy.
Love is not rude or arrogant,
It is not puffed up, it behaves without resentment.
Love rejoices at truthfulness;
It endures all things, believes all things,
It hopes all thing, suffers all things.
Unceasing love never fails."
(I Corinthians 13:1-8a)

REFRAIN (CHILDREN'S CHOIR):

We have a future:
We children have a future
if we're always human creatures.
Humans with our minds and hearts.
No, not discrimination and exploitation, not sexual abuse.
Let us humans be humane!
Live! Live! Live in love!

We boys have a future.
We girls have a future.
We children have a future, if we're always human,
humans with our minds and hearts.
Let us humans human be

CHOIR:
A human without humanity,
What use are the rituals?

(Golden Rule)
Do not do to others,
what you don't want
done to you.
(Rabbi Hillel, Sabbath 31a)

Whoever is born for a divine destiny...
the destiny divine leads to redemption
(Mahabharata VI, 40, 5)

SPEAKER:
Live. Live in Peace!
Humanity.
In Freedom.
Justice.
Truthfulness.
Live in Love.
Live.

CHOIR: (solo basses)
Love seeks not its own ends, is not easily provoked.

CHOIR:

An ethos of justice is the message of the Prophet.
(Muhammad)

He saw through suffering and what suffering brings:
Greed, hate, and blindness.
(Buddha)

Unceasing love never fails.
It counts not evil in.
It rejoices not over injustice.
(Paul)

Freedom! Peace! Love!

IV.

Global Ethic Documents

1. Declaration Toward a Global Ethic by the Parliament of the World's Religions
   (Chicago, September 4, 1993)

Introduction

[The text entitled 'Introduction' was produced by an Editorial Committee of the Council of the Parliament of the World's Religions in Chicago on the basis of the declaration itself composed in Tübingen (here headed 'Principles'). It was meant to serve as a brief summary of the declaration for publicity purposes.]

The world is in agony. The agony is so pervasive and urgent that we are compelled to name its manifestations so that the depth of this pain may be made clear.

Peace eludes us—the planet is being destroyed—neighbors live in fear—women and men are estranged from each other —children die! This is abhorrent.

We condemn the abuses of Earth's ecosystems.

We condemn the poverty that stifles life's potential; the hunger that weakens the human body, the economic disparities that threaten so many families with ruin.

We condemn the social disarray of the nations; the disregard for justice which pushes citizens to the margin; the anarchy overtaking our communities; and the insane death of children from violence. In particular we condemn aggression and hatred in the name of religion.

But this agony need not be.

It need not be because the basis for an ethic already exists. This ethic offers the possibility of a better individual and global order, and leads individuals away from despair and societies away from chaos.

We are women and men who have embraced the precepts and practices of the world's religions:

We affirm that a common set of core values is found in the teachings of the religions, and that these form the basis of a global ethic.

We affirm that this truth is already known, but yet to be lived in heart and action.

We affirm that there is an irrevocable, unconditional norm for all areas of life, for families and communities, for races, nations, and religions. There already exist ancient guidelines for human behavior which are found in the teachings of the religions of the world and which are the condition for a sustainable world order.

We declare:

We are interdependent. Each of us depends on the well-being of the whole, and so we have respect for the community of living beings, for people, animals, and plants, and for the preservation of Earth, the air, water and soil.

We take individual responsibility for all we do. All our decisions, actions, and failures to act have consequences.

We must treat others as we wish others to treat us. We make a commitment to respect life and dignity, individuality and diversity, so that every person is treated humanely, without exception.

We must have patience and acceptance. We must be able to forgive, learning from the past but never allowing ourselves to be enslaved by memories of hate. Opening our hearts to one another, we must sink our narrow differences for the cause of the world community, practicing a culture of solidarity and relatedness.

We consider humankind our family. We must strive to be kind and generous. We must not live for ourselves alone, but should also serve others, never forgetting the children, the aged, the poor, the suffering, the disabled, the refugees, and the lonely. No person should ever be considered or treated as a second-class citizen, or be exploited in any way whatsoever. There should be equal partnership between men and women.

We must not commit any kind of sexual immorality. We must put behind us all forms of domination or abuse.

We commit ourselves to a culture of nonviolence, respect, justice, and peace. We shall not oppress, injure, torture, or kill other human beings, forsaking violence as a means of settling differences.

We must strive for a just social and economic order, in which everyone has an equal chance to reach full potential as a human being. We must speak and act truthfully and with compassion, dealing fairly with all, and avoiding prejudice and hatred. We must not steal. We must move beyond the dominance of greed for power, prestige, money, and consumption to make a just and peaceful world.

Earth cannot be changed for the better unless the consciousness of individuals is changed first. We pledge to increase our awareness by disciplining our minds, by meditation, by prayer, or by positive thinking. Without risk and a readiness to sacrifice there can be no fundamental change in our situation. Therefore we commit ourselves to this global ethic, to understanding one another, and to socially beneficial, peace-fostering, and nature-friendly ways of life. We invite all people, whether religious or not, to do the same.

1. The Principles of a Global Ethic

Our world is experiencing a *fundamental crisis*: A crisis in the global economy, global ecology, and global politics. The lack of a grand vision, the tangle of unresolved problems, political paralysis, mediocre political leadership with little insight or foresight, and in general too little sense for the commonweal are seen everywhere: Too many old answers to new challenges.

Hundreds of millions of human beings on our planet increasingly suffer from unemployment, poverty, hunger, and the destruction of their families. Hope for a lasting peace among nations eludes us. There are tensions between the sexes and generations. Children die, kill, and are killed. More and more countries are shaken by corruption in politics and business. It is increasingly difficult to live together peacefully in our cities because of social, racial, and ethnic conflicts, the abuse of drugs, organized crime, and even anarchy. Even neighbors often live in fear of one another. Our planet continues to be ruthlessly plundered. A collapse of the ecosystem threatens us.

Time and again we see leaders and members of religions incite aggression, fanaticism, hate, and xenophobia—even inspire and legitimize violent and bloody conflicts. Religion often is misused for purely power-political goals, including war. We are filled with disgust.

We condemn these blights and declare that they need not be. An ethic already exists within the religious teachings of the world which can counter the global distress. Of course, this ethic provides no direct solution for all the immense problems of the world, but it does supply the moral foundation for a better individual and global order: A vision that can lead women and men away from despair, and society away from chaos.

We are persons who have committed ourselves to the precepts and practices of the world's religions. We confirm that there is already a consensus among the religions which can be the basis for a global ethic—a minimal fundamental consensus concerning binding values, irrevocable standards, and fundamental moral attitudes.

I. No new global order without a new global ethic!

We women and men of various religions and regions of Earth therefore address all people, religious and nonreligious. We wish to express the following convictions which we hold in common:

- We all have a responsibility for a better global order.

- Our involvement for the sake of human rights, freedom, justice, peace, and the preservation of Earth is absolutely necessary.

- Our different religious and cultural traditions must not prevent our common involvement in opposing all forms of inhumanity and working for greater humaneness.

- The principles expressed in this Global Ethic can be affirmed by all persons with ethical convictions, whether religiously grounded or not.

- As religious and spiritual persons we base our lives on an Ultimate Reality and draw spiritual power and hope therefrom, in trust, in prayer or meditation, in word or silence. We have a special responsibility for the welfare of all humanity and care for the planet Earth. We do not consider ourselves better than other women and men, we simply trust that the ancient wisdom of our religions can point the way for the future.

After two world wars and the end of the Cold War, the collapse of fascism and Nazism, the shaking to the foundations of communism and colonialism, humanity has entered a new phase of history. Today we possess sufficient economic, cultural, and spiritual resources to introduce a better global order. But old and new *ethnic, national, social, economic, and religious tensions* threaten the peaceful building of a better world. We have experienced greater technological progress than ever before, yet we see that worldwide poverty, hunger, death of children, unemployment, misery, and the destruction of nature have not diminished but rather increased. Many peoples are threatened with economic ruin, social disarray, political marginalization, ecological catastrophe, and national collapse.

In such a dramatic global situation humanity needs a vision of peoples living peacefully together, of ethnic and ethical groupings, and of religions sharing responsibility for the care of Earth. The vision rests on hopes, goals, ideals, and standards. But all over the world, these have slipped from our hands. Yet we are convinced that, despite their frequent abuses and failures, it is the communities of faith who bear a responsibility to demonstrate that such hopes, ideals, and standards can be guarded, grounded, and lived. This is especially true in the modern state. Guarantees of freedom of conscience and religion are necessary but they do not substitute for binding values, convictions, and norms that are valid for all humans regardless of their social origin, sex, skin color, language, or religion.

We are convinced of the fundamental unity of the human family on Earth. We recall the 1948 Universal Declaration of Human Rights of the United Nations. What it formally proclaimed on the level of rights we wish to confirm and deepen here from the perspective of an ethic: The full realization of the intrinsic dignity of the human person, the inalienable freedom and equality in principle of all humans, and the necessary solidarity and interdependence of all humans with each other.

On the basis of personal experiences and the burdensome history of our planet we have learned:

- that a better global order cannot be created or enforced by laws, prescriptions, and conventions alone;

- that the realization of peace, justice, and the protection of Earth depends on the insight and readiness of men and women to act justly;

- that action in favor of rights and freedoms presumes a consciousness of responsibility and duty, and therefore both the minds and hearts of women and men must be addressed;

- that rights without morality cannot long endure, and that there will be no better global order without a global ethic.

By a global ethic we do not mean a global ideology or a single unified religion beyond all existing religions, and certainly not the domination of one religion over all others. By a global ethic we mean a fundamental consensus on binding values, irrevocable standards, and personal attitudes. Without such a fundamental consensus on an ethic, sooner or later every community will be threatened by chaos or dictatorship, and individuals will despair.

II. A fundamental demand:

Every human being must be treated humanely.

We are all fallible, imperfect men and women with limitations and defects. We know the reality of evil. Precisely because of this, we feel compelled for the sake of global welfare to express what the fundamental elements of a global ethic should be—for individuals as well as for communities and organizations, for states as well as for the religions themselves. We trust that our often millennia-old religious and ethical traditions provide an ethic that is convincing and practicable for all women and men of goodwill, religious and nonreligious.

At the same time, we know that our various religious and ethical traditions often offer very different bases for what is helpful and unhelpful for men and women, what is right and wrong, what is good and evil. We do not wish to gloss over or ignore the serious differences among the individual religions. However, they should not hinder us from proclaiming publicly those things which we already hold in common and which we jointly affirm, each on the basis of our own religious or ethical grounds.

We know that religions cannot solve the environmental, economic, political, and social problems of Earth. However, they can provide what obviously cannot be attained by economic plans, political programs, or legal regulations alone: A change in the inner orientation, the whole mentality, the hearts of people, and a conversion from a false path to a new orientation for life. Humankind urgently needs social and ecological reforms, but it needs spiritual renewal just as urgently. As religious or spiritual persons we commit ourselves to this task. The spiritual powers of the religions can offer a fundamental sense of trust, a ground of

165

meaning, ultimate standards, and a spiritual home. Of course religions are credible only when they eliminate those conflicts which spring from the religions themselves, dismantling mutual arrogance, mistrust, prejudice, and even hostility, and thus demonstrate respect for the traditions, holy places, feasts, and rituals of people who believe differently.

Now as before, women and men are treated inhumanely all over the world. They are robbed of their opportunities and their freedom; their human rights are trampled underfoot; their dignity is disregarded. But might does not make right! In the face of all inhumanity, our religious and ethical convictions demand that every human being must be treated humanely!

This means that every human being without distinction of age, sex, race, skin color, physical or mental ability, language, religion, political view, or national or social origin possesses an inalienable and untouchable dignity, and everyone, the individual as well as the state, is therefore obliged to honor and protect this dignity. Humans must always be the subjects of rights. They must be ends, never mere means, never objects of commercialization and industrialization in economics, politics, and media, in research institutes, and industrial corporations. No one stands above good and evil—no human being, no social class, no influential interest group, no cartel, no police apparatus, no army, and no state. On the contrary, possessed of reason and conscience, every human is obliged to behave in a genuinely human fashion, to do good and avoid evil!

It is the intention of this Global Ethic to clarify what this means. In it, we wish to recall irrevocable, unconditional ethical norms. These should not be bonds and chains, but helps and supports for people to find and realize once again their lives' direction, values, orientations, and meaning.

There is a principle which is found and has persisted in many religious and ethical traditions of humankind for thousands of years: *What you do not wish done to yourself, do not do to others.* Or in positive terms: *What you wish done to yourself, do to others!* This should be the irrevocable, unconditional norm for all areas of life, for families and communities, for races, nations, and religions.

Every form of egoism should be rejected: all selfishness, whether individual or collective, whether in the form of class thinking, racism, nationalism, or sexism. We condemn these because they prevent humans from being authentically human. Self-determination and self-realization are thoroughly legitimate so long as they are not separated from human self-responsibility and global responsibility, that is, from responsibility for fellow humans and for the planet Earth.

This principle implies very concrete standards to which we humans should hold firm. From it arise four broad, ancient guidelines for human behavior which are found in most of the religions of the world.

III. Irrevocable directives

1. Commitment to a Culture of Nonviolence and Respect for Life

Numerous women and men of all regions and religions strive to lead lives not determined by egoism but by commitment to their fellow humans and to the world around them. Nevertheless, all over the world we find endless hatred, envy, jealousy, and violence, not only between individuals but between social and

167

ethnic groups, classes, races, nations, and religions. The use of violence, drug trafficking, and organized crime, often equipped with new technical possibilities, has reached global proportions. Many places are still ruled by terror from above; dictators oppress their own people, and institutional violence is widespread. Even in some countries where laws exist to protect individual freedoms, prisoners are tortured, men and women are mutilated, and hostages are killed.

A. In the great ancient religious and ethical traditions of humankind we find the directive: You shall not kill! Or in positive terms: Have respect for life! Let us reflect anew on the consequences of this ancient directive: All people have a right to life, safety, and the free development of personality insofar as they do not injure the rights of others. No one has the right physically or psychically to torture or injure, much less kill, any other human being. And no people, state, race, or religion has the right to hate, to discriminate against, to cleanse, to exile, much less to liquidate a foreign minority which is different in behavior or holds different beliefs.

B. Of course, wherever there are humans there will be conflicts. Such conflicts, however, should be resolved without violence within a framework of justice. This is true for states as well as individuals. Persons who hold political power must work within the framework of a just order and commit themselves to the most nonviolent, peaceful solutions possible. They should work toward answers within an international order of peace which itself has need of protection and defense against perpetrators of violence. Armament is a mistaken path; disarmament is the sentiment of the times. Let no one be deceived: there is no survival for humanity without global peace!

C. Young people must learn at home and in school that violence may not be a means of settling differences with others. Only thus can a *culture of nonviolence* be created.

D. A human person is infinitely precious and must be unconditionally protected. But likewise the lives of animals and plants which inhabit this planet with us deserve protection, preservation, and care. Limitless exploitation of the natural foundations of life, ruthless destruction of the biosphere, and militarization of the cosmos are all outrages. As human beings we have a special responsibility—especially with a view to future generations—for Earth and the cosmos, for the air, water, and soil. We are all intertwined together in this cosmos and dependent on each other. Each one of us depends on the welfare of all. Therefore the dominance of humanity over nature and the cosmos must not be encouraged. Instead we must cultivate living in harmony with nature and the universe.

E. To be authentically human in the spirit of our great religious and ethical tradition means that in public as well as in private life we must be concerned for others and ready to help. We must never be ruthless and brutal. Every people, every race, and every religion must show tolerance and respect—indeed high appreciation—for every other. Minorities need protection and support, whether they be racial, ethnic, or religious.

2. Commitment to a Culture of Solidarity and a Just Economic Order

Numberless men and women of all regions and religions strive to live their lives in solidarity with one another and to work for authentic fulfillment of their vocations. Nevertheless, all over the world we find endless hunger, deficiency, and need. Not only individuals, but especially unjust institutions and structures are responsible for these tragedies. Millions of people are without work; millions are exploited by poor wages, forced to the edges of society, with their possibilities for the future destroyed. In many lands the gap between the poor and the rich, between the powerful and the powerless is immense. We live in a world in which totalitarian state socialism as well as unbridled capitalism have hollowed out and destroyed many ethical and spiritual values. A materialistic mentality breeds greed for unlimited profit and a grasping for endless plunder. These demands claim more and more of the community's resources without obliging the individual to contribute more. The cancerous social evil of corruption thrives in developing countries and developed countries alike.

A. In the great ancient religious and ethical traditions of humankind we find the directive: You shall not steal! Or in positive terms: Deal honestly and fairly! Let us reflect anew on the consequences of this ancient directive: No one has the right to rob or dispossess in any way whatsoever any other person or the commonweal. Further, no one has the right to use her or his possessions without concern for the needs of society and Earth.

B. Where extreme poverty reigns, helplessness and despair spread and theft occurs again and again for the sake of survival. Where power and wealth are accumulated ruthlessly, feelings of envy, resentment, and deadly hatred and rebellion inevitably well up in the disadvantaged and marginalized. This leads to a vicious circle of violence and counterviolence. Let no one be deceived: there is no global peace without global justice!

C. Young people must learn at home and in school that property, limited though it may be, carries with it an obligation, and that its uses should at the same time serve the common good. Only thus can a just economic order be built.

D. If the plight of the poorest billions of humans on this planet, particularly women and children, is to be improved, the world economy must be structured more justly. Individual good deeds and assistance projects, indispensable though they be, are insufficient. The participation of all states and the authority of international organizations are needed to build just economic institutions.

A solution which can be supported by all sides must be sought for the debt crisis and the poverty of the dissolving second world, and even more the third world. Of course conflicts of interest are unavoidable. In the developed countries, a distinction must be made between necessary and limitless consumption, between socially beneficial and unbeneficial uses of property, between justified and unjustified uses of natural resources, and between a profit-only and a socially beneficial and ecologically oriented market economy. Even the developing nations must search their national consciences.

Wherever those ruling threaten to repress those ruled, wherever institutions threaten persons, and wherever might oppresses right, we are obligated to resist—whenever possible, nonviolently.

E. To be authentically human in the spirit of our great religious and ethical traditions means the following:

- We must utilize economic and political power for service to humanity instead of misusing it in ruthless battles for domination. We must develop a spirit of compassion for those who suffer, with special care for the children, the aged, the poor, the disabled, the refugees, and the lonely.

- We must cultivate mutual respect and consideration, so as to reach a reasonable balance of interests instead of thinking only of unlimited power and unavoidable competitive struggles.

- We must value a sense of moderation and modesty instead of an unquenchable greed for money, prestige, and consumption. In greed humans lose their souls, their freedom, their composure, their inner peace, and thus that which makes them human.

3. Commitment to a Culture of Tolerance and a Life of Truthfulness

Numerous women and men of all regions and religions strive to lead lives of honesty and truthfulness. Nevertheless, all over the world we find endless lies, deceit, swindling and hypocrisy, ideology, and demagoguery:

- Politicians and business people who use lies as a means to success;

- Mass media which spread ideological propaganda instead of accurate reporting, misinformation instead of information, cynical commercial interest instead of loyalty to the truth;

- Scientists and researchers who give themselves over to morally questionable ideological or political programs or to economic interest groups, or who justify research which violates fundamental ethical values;

- Representatives of religions who dismiss other religions as of little value and who preach fanaticism and intolerance instead of respect and understanding.

A. In the great ancient religious and ethical traditions of humankind we find the directive: You shall not lie! Or in positive terms: Speak and act truthfully! Let us reflect anew on the consequences of this ancient directive: No woman or man, institution, state, church, or religious community has the right to speak lies to other humans.

B. This is especially true:

- for those who work in the *mass media* to whom we entrust the freedom to report for the sake of truth and to whom we thus grant the office of guardian. They do not stand above morality but have the obligation to respect human dignity, human rights, and fundamental values. They are duty-bound to objectivity, fairness, and the preservation of human dignity. They have no right to intrude into individuals' private spheres, to manipulate public opinion, or distort reality;

- for *artists, writers,* and *scientists* to whom we entrust artistic and academic freedom. They are not exempt from general ethical standards and must serve the truth;

- for the leaders of countries, *politicians,* and *political parties* to whom we entrust our own freedoms. When they lie in the faces of their people, when they manipulate the truth, or when they are guilty of venality or ruthlessness in domestic or foreign affairs, they forsake their credibility and deserve to lose their offices and their voters. Conversely, public opinion should support those politicians who dare to speak the truth to people at all times;

- finally, for *representatives of religion*. When they stir up prejudice, hatred, and enmity towards those of different belief or incite or legitimize religious wars, they deserve the condemnation of humankind and the loss of their adherents.

Let no one be deceived: There is no global justice without truthfulness and humaneness!

C. Young people must learn at home and in school to think, speak, and act truthfully. They have a right to information and education to be able to make the decisions that will form their lives. Without an ethical formation they will hardly be able to distinguish the important from the unimportant. In the daily flood of information, ethical standards will help them discern when opinions are portrayed as facts, interests veiled, tendencies exaggerated, and facts twisted.

D. To be authentically human in the spirit of our great religious and ethical traditions means the following:

- We must not confuse freedom with arbitrariness or pluralism with indifference to truth.

- We must cultivate truthfulness in all our relationships instead of dishonesty, dissembling, and opportunism.

- We must constantly seek truth and incorruptible sincerity instead of spreading ideological or partisan half-truths.

- We must courageously serve the truth and remain constant and trustworthy, instead of yielding to an opportunistic accommodation to life.

4. Commitment to a Culture of Equal Rights and Partnership Between Men and Women

Numberless men and women of all regions and religions strive to live their lives in a spirit of partnership and responsible action in the areas of love, sexuality, and family. Nevertheless, all over the world there are condemnable forms of patriarchy, domination of one sex over the other, exploitation of women, sexual misuse of children, and forced prostitution. Too frequently, social inequities force women and even children into prostitution as a means of survival—particularly in less developed countries.

A. In the great ancient religious and ethical traditions of humankind we find the directive: *You shall not commit sexual immorality!* Or in positive terms: *Respect and love one another!* Let us reflect anew on the consequences of this ancient directive: No one has the right to degrade others to mere sex objects, to lead them into—or hold them—in sexual dependency.

B. We condemn sexual exploitation and sexual discrimination as one of the worst forms of human degradation. We have the duty to resist wherever the domination of one sex over the other is preached—even in the name of religious conviction; wherever sexual exploitation is tolerated, wherever prostitution is fostered or children are misused. Let no one be deceived: There is no authentic humaneness without living together in partnership!

C. Young people must learn at home and in school that sexuality is not a negative, destructive, or exploitative force, but creative and affirmative. Sexuality as a life-affirming shaper of community can only be effective when partners accept the responsibilities of caring for one another's happiness.

D. The relationship between women and men should be characterized not by patronizing behavior or exploitation, but by love, partnership, and trustworthiness. Human fulfillment is not identical with sexual pleasure. Sexuality should express and reinforce a loving relationship lived by equal partners.

Some religious traditions know the ideal of a voluntary renunciation of the full use of sexuality. Voluntary renunciation can also be an expression of identity and meaningful fulfillment.

E. The social institution of marriage, despite all its cultural and religious variety, is characterized by love, loyalty, and permanence. It aims at and should guarantee security and mutual support to husband, wife, and child. It should secure the rights of all family members. All lands and cultures should develop economic and social relationships which will enable marriage and family life worthy of human beings, especially for older people. Children have a right of access to education. Parents should not exploit children, nor children, parents. Their relationships should reflect mutual respect, appreciation, and concern.

F. To be authentically human in the spirit of our great religious and ethical traditions means the following:

- We need mutual respect, partnership, and understanding instead of patriarchal domination and degradation, which are expressions of violence and engender counter violence.

- We need mutual concern, tolerance, readiness for reconciliation, and love instead of any form of possessive lust or sexual misuse.

Only what has already been experienced in personal and familial relationships can be practiced on the level of nations and religions.

5. Commitment to a Culture of Sustainability and Care for the Earth

(added by the Toronto Parliament of the World's Religions, November 2018)

Numberless men and women of all regions and religions strive to lead lives in a spirit of mutual harmony, interdependence, and respect for the Earth, its living beings and ecosystems. Nevertheless, in most parts of the world, pollution contaminates the soil, air, and water; deforestation and overreliance on fossil fuels contribute to climate change; habitats are destroyed, and species are fished or hunted to extinction. Overexploitation and unjust use of natural resources increases conflict and poverty among people and harms other forms of life. Too often, the poorest populations, though they have the smallest impact, bear the brunt of the damage done to the planet's atmosphere, land, and oceans.

A. In the religious, spiritual, and cultural traditions of humankind we find the directive: You shall not be greedy! Or in positive terms: remember the good of all! Let us reflect anew on the consequences of this directive: we should help provide—to the best of our ability—for the needs and well-being of others, including today's and tomorrow's children. The Earth, with its finite resources, is shared by our one human family. It sustains us and many forms of life, and calls for our respect and care. Many religious, spiritual, and cultural traditions place us within the interdependent web of life; at the same time, they accord us a distinctive role and affirm that our gifts of knowledge and craft place upon us the obligation to use these gifts wisely to foster the common good.

B. All of us have the responsibility to minimize, as much as we can, our impact on the Earth, to refrain from treating living beings and the environment as mere things for personal use and enjoyment, and to consider the effects of our actions on future generations. Caring and prudent use of resources is based on fairness in consumption and considers limits on what ecosystems can bear. Wherever heedless domination by human beings over the Earth and other living beings is taught, wherever abuse of the environment is tolerated, and wherever development surpasses sustainable limits, we have the duty to speak up, to change our practices, and to moderate our lifestyles.

C. Young people should be encouraged to appreciate that a good life is not a life of outsized consumption or amassing material possessions. A good life strikes a balance between one's needs, the needs of others, and the health of the planet. Education about the environment and sustainable living should become part of the school curricula in every country of the world.

D. To be authentically human in the spirit of our religious, spiritual, and cultural traditions means the following: our relationship with each other and with the larger living world should be based on respect, care, and gratitude. All traditions teach that the Earth is a source of wonder and wisdom. Its vitality, diversity, and beauty are held in trust for everyone including those who will come after us. The global environmental crisis is urgent and is deepening. The planet and its countless forms of life are in danger. Time is running out. We must act with love and compassion—for justice and fairness—for the flourishing of the whole Earth community.

IV. A Transformation of Consciousness

Historical experience demonstrates the following: Earth cannot be changed for the better unless we achieve a transformation in the consciousness of individuals and in public life. The possibilities for transformation have already been glimpsed in areas such as war and peace, economy, and ecology, where in recent decades fundamental changes have taken place. This transformation must also be achieved in the area of ethics and values!

Every individual has intrinsic dignity and inalienable rights, and each also has an inescapable responsibility for what she or he does and does not do. All our decisions and deeds, even our omissions and failures, have consequences.
Keeping this sense of responsibility alive, deepening it, and passing it on to future generations is the special task of religions.

We are realistic about what we have achieved in this consensus, and so we urge that the following be observed:

- A universal consensus on many disputed ethical questions (from bio- and sexual ethics, mass media and scientific ethics, to economic and political ethics) will be difficult to attain. Nevertheless, even for many controversial questions, suitable solutions should be attainable in the spirit of the fundamental principles we have jointly developed here.

- In many areas of life a new consciousness of ethical responsibility has already arisen. Therefore we would be pleased if as many professions as possible, such as those of physicians, scientists, business people, journalists, and politicians would develop up-to-date codes of ethics which would provide specific guidelines for the vexing questions of these particular professions.

- Above all, we urge the various communities of faith to formulate their very specific ethics. What does each faith tradition have to say, for example, about the meaning of life and death, the enduring of suffering, and the forgiveness of guilt, about selfless sacrifice and the necessity of renunciation, about compassion and joy? These will deepen, and make more specific, the already discernible global ethic.

In conclusion, we appeal to all the inhabitants of this planet. Earth cannot be changed for the better unless the consciousness of individuals is changed. We pledge to work for such transformation in individual and collective consciousness, for the awakening of our spiritual powers through reflection, meditation, prayer, or positive thinking, for a *conversion of the heart*. Together we can move mountains! Without a willingness to take risks and a readiness to sacrifice there can be no fundamental change in our situation! Therefore we commit ourselves to a common global ethic, to better mutual understanding as well as to socially beneficial, peace-fostering, and Earth-friendly ways of life.

We invite all men and women, whether religious or not, to do the same!

This declaration was signed by around 200 delegates of the Parliament of the World's Religions. Among them were such prominent persons as the Dalai Lama and the Cardinal of Chicago, representatives of the World Council of Churches and the President of the Lutheran World Federation, the General Secretary of the World Conference of Religions for Peace and the Secretary-General of the Bahá'i International Community, the spiritual head of the Sikh religion in Amritsar, a leading figure of Cambodian Buddhism, an eminent rabbi, a leading Muslim feminist, and many others beside.

2. Proposal of the InterAction Council of Former Heads of State and Government for a Universal Declaration of Human Responsibilities (1997)

Preamble

Whereas recognition of the inherent dignity and of the equal and inalienable rights of all members of the human family is the foundation of freedom, justice, and peace in the world and implies obligations or responsibilities,

Whereas the exclusive insistence on rights can result in conflict, division, and endless dispute, and the neglect of human responsibilities can lead to lawlessness and chaos,

Whereas the rule of law and the promotion of human rights depend on the readiness of men and women to act justly,

Whereas global problems demand global solutions which can only be achieved through ideas, values, and norms respected by all cultures and societies,

Whereas all people, to the best of their knowledge and ability, have a responsibility to foster a better social order, both at home and globally, a goal which cannot be achieved by laws, prescriptions, and conventions alone,

Whereas human aspirations for progress and improvement can only be realized by agreed upon values and standards applying to all people and institutions at all times,

Now, therefore,
The General Assembly

proclaims this Universal Declaration of Human Responsibilities as a common standard for all peoples and all nations, to the end that every individual and every organ of society, keeping this Declaration constantly in mind, shall contribute to the advancement of communities and the enlightenment of all their members. We the peoples of the world thus renew and reinforce commitments already proclaimed in the Universal Declaration of Human Rights, namely the full acceptance of the dignity of all people; their inalienable freedom and equality, and their solidarity with another. Awareness and acceptance of these responsibilities should be taught and promoted throughout the world.

Fundamental Principles for Humanity

Article 1
Every person, regardless of gender, ethnic origin, social status, political opinion, language, age, nationality, or religion **has a responsibility to treat all people in a humane way**.

Article 2

No person should lend support to any form of inhumane behavior, but all people have a responsibility to strive for the dignity and self-esteem of all others.

Article 3

No person, no group or organization, state, army, or police force stands above good and evil; all are subject to ethical standards. Everyone has a responsibility to promote good and to avoid evil in all things.

Article 4

All people endowed with reason and conscience must accept a responsibility to each and all, to families and communities, to races, nations, and religions in a spirit of solidarity: What you do not wish to be done to yourself, do not do to others.

Nonviolence and Respect for Life

Article 5

Every person has a responsibility to respect life. No one has the right to injure, to torture, or to kill another human person. This does not exclude the right of justified self-defense of individuals or communities.

Article 6

Disputes between states, groups, or individuals should be resolved without violence. No government should tolerate or participate in acts of genocide or terrorism, nor should it abuse women, children, or any other civilians as instruments of war. Every citizen and public official has a responsibility to act in a peaceful, nonviolent way.

Article 7

Every person is infinitely precious and must be protected unconditionally. The animals and the natural environment also demand protection. All people have a responsibility to protect the air, water, and soil for the sake of present inhabitants and future generations.

Justice and Solidarity

Article 8

Every person has a responsibility to behave with integrity, honesty, and fairness. No person or group should rob or arbitrarily deprive any other person or group of their property.

Article 9

All people, given the necessary tools, have a responsibility to make serious efforts to overcome poverty, malnutrition, ignorance, and inequality. They should promote sustainable development all over the world in order to assure dignity, freedom, security, and justice for all people.

Article 10

All people have a responsibility to develop their talents through diligent endeavor; they should have equal access to education and meaningful work. Everyone should lend support to the needy, the disadvantaged, the disabled, and victims of discrimination.

Article 11

All property and wealth must be used responsibly in accordance with justice and for the advancement of the human race. Economic and political power must not be handled as an instrument of domination, but in the service of economic justice and the social order.

Truthfulness and Tolerance

Article 12
Every person has a responsibility to speak and act truthfully. No one, however elite, should speak lies. The right to privacy and to personal and professional confidentiality is to be respected. No one is obliged to tell all the truth to everyone all the time.

Article 13
No politicians, public servants, business leaders, scientists, writers, or artists are exempt from general ethical standards; nor are physicians, lawyers, and other professionals who have special duties to clients. Professional and other codes of ethics should reflect the priority of general standards such as those of truthfulness and fairness.

Article 14
The freedom of the media to inform the public and criticize institutions of society and governmental actions, which is essential for a just society, must be used with responsibility and discretion. Freedom of the media carries a special responsibility for accurate and truthful reporting. Sensational reporting that degrades the human person or dignity must at all times be avoided.

Article 15
While religious freedom must be guaranteed, the representatives of religions have a special responsibility to avoid expressions of prejudice and acts of discrimination toward those of different beliefs. They should not incite or legitimize hatred, fanaticism, or religious wars, but should foster tolerance and mutual respect between all people.

Mutual Respect and Partnership

Article 16

All men and women have a responsibility to show respect to one another and understanding in their partnership. No one should subject another person to sexual exploitation or dependence. Rather, sexual partners should accept the responsibility of caring for each other's well-being.

Article 17

In all its cultural and religious varieties, marriage requires love, loyalty, and forgiveness and should aim at guaranteeing security and mutual support.

Article 18

Sensible family planning is the responsibility of every couple. The relationship between parents and children should reflect mutual love, respect, appreciation, and concern. No parents or other adults should exploit, abuse, or maltreat children.

Conclusion

Article 19

Nothing in this Declaration may be interpreted as implying for any state, group, or person any right to engage in any activity or to perform any act aimed at the destruction of any of the responsibilities, rights, and freedoms set forth in this Declaration and in the Universal Declaration of Human Rights of 1948.

Endorsement of the Declaration

The proposed Universal Declaration of Human Responsibilities have the endorsement of the following individuals:

I. The InterAction Council Members

Helmut Schmidt
Former Chancellor of the Federal Republic of Germany
Malcolm Fraser (Chair)
Former Prime Minister of Australia
Andries A. M. van Agt
Former Prime Minister of the Netherlands
Anand Panyarachun
Former Prime Minister of Thailand
Óscar Arias Sánchez
Former President to of Costa Rica
Lord Callaghan of Cardiff
Former Prime Minister of the United Kingdom
Jimmy Carter
Former President of the United States
Miguel de la Madrid Hurtado
Former President of Mexico
Kurt Furgler
Former President of Switzerland
Valéry Giscard d'Estaing
Former President of France
Felipe Gonzalez Marquez
Former Prime Minister of Spain
Mikhail S. Gorbachev
Chair of the Supreme Soviet and
President of the Union of Soviet Socialist Republics

Selim Hoss
Former Prime Minister of Lebanon
Kenneth Kaunda
Former President of Zambia
Lee Kuan Yew
Former Prime Minister of Singapore
Kiichi Miyazawa
Former Prime Minister of Japan
Misael Pastrana Borrero
Former President of Colombia (deceased in August 2019)
Shimon Peres
Former Prime Minister of Israel
Maria de Lourdes Pintasilgo
Former Prime Minister of Portugal
Jose Sarney
Former President of Brazil
Shin Hyon Hwak
Former Prime Minister of the Republic of Korea
Kalevi Sorsa
Former Prime Minister of Finland
Pierre Elliott Trudeau
Former Prime Minister of Canada
Ola Ullsten
Former Prime Minister of Sweden
George Vassiliou
Former President of Cyprus
Franz Vranitzky
Former President of Austria

II. Supporters

Ali Alatas, Minister for Foreign Affairs, Indonesia
Abdulaziz Al-Quraishi, former Chair of SAMA
Lester Brown, President, Worldwatch Institute
Andre Chouraqui, Professor in Israel (deceased in July 2007)
John B. Cobb Jr., Claremont School of Theology
Takako Doi, President, Japan Socialist Democratic Party
Kan Kato, President, Chiba University of Commerce
Henry A. Kissinger, Former U.S. Secretary of State
Teddy Kollek, Mayor of Jerusalem
William Laughlin, American entrepreneur
Chwasan Lee Kwang Jung,
Head Dharma Master, Won Buddhism
Federico Mayor, Director-General, UNESCO
Robert S. McNamara, former President, World Bank
Rabbi Dr. J.Magonet, Principal, Leo Baek College
Robert Muller, Rector, University for Peace
Konrad Raiser, World Council of Churches
Jonathan Sacks, Chief Rabbi of the UK
Seijuro Shiokawa, former Ministers of Home Affairs, Education
and Transportation of Japan
Rene Samuel Sirat, Chief Rabbi of France
Sir Sigmund Sternberg,
International Council of Christians and Jews
Masayoshi Takemura, former Finance Minister of Japan
Gaston Thorn, former Prime Minister of Luxembourg
Paul Volcker, Chair, James D. Wolfensohn Inc.
Carl Friedrich v. Weizsäcker, Scientist
Richard v. Weizsäcker,
former President of the Federal Republic of Germany
Mahmoud Zakzouk, Minister of Religion, Egypt

III. Participants (in preparatory meetings in Vienna, Austria in March 1996 and April 1997) and special guests (at the 15th Plenary Session in Noordwijk, The Netherlands in June 1997)

Hans Küng, Tubingen University
(academic advisor to the project)
Thomas Axworthy, CRB Foundation
(academic advisor to the project)
Kim, Kyong-Dong, Seoul National University
(academic advisor to the project)
Cardinal Franz Koenig, Vienna, Austria
Anna-Marie Aagaard, World Council of Churches
A.A. Mughram Al-Ghamdi, The King Fahad Academy
M. Aram, World Conference on Religion & Peace
A.T. Ariyaratne, Sarvodaya Movement of Sri Lanka
Julia Ching, University of Toronto
Hassan Hanafi, University of Cairo
Nagaharu Hayabusa, The Asahi Shimbun
Yersu Kim, Division of Philosophy and Ethics, UNESCO
Peter Landesmann, European Academy of Sciences
Lee, Seung-Yun, Former Deputy Prime Minister and Minister of
Economic Planning Board of the Republic of Korea
Flora Lewis, International Herald Tribune
Liu, Xiaofeng, Institute of Sino-Christian Studies
Teri McLuhan, Canadian author
Isamu Miyazaki, Former State Minister,
Economic Planning Agency of Japan
J.J.N. Rost Onnes, Executive Vice President, ABN AMRO Bank
James Ottley,
Anglican Observer at the United Nations
Richard Rorty, Stanford Humanities Center
L. M. Singhvi, High Commissioner for India
Marjorie Hewitt Suchocki, Claremont School of Theology

Seiken Sugiura, House of Representatives of Japan
Koji Watanabe, Former Japanese Ambassador to Russia
Woo, Seong-yong, Munhwa Ilbo
Wu Xueqian, Vice Chair,
Chinese People's Political Consultative Conference
Alexander Yakovlev, Former Member,
Presidential Council of the Soviet Union

3. Manifesto for a Global Economic Ethic. Consequences for the Global Economy (2009)

Preamble

For the globalization of economic activity to lead to universal and sustainable prosperity, all those who either take part in or are affected by economic activities are dependent on a values-based commercial exchange and cooperation. This is one of the fundamental lessons of today's worldwide crisis of the financial and product markets.

Further, fair commercial exchange and cooperation will only achieve sustainable societal goals when people's activities to realize their legitimate private interests and prosperity are imbedded in a global ethical framework that enjoys broad acceptance. Such an agreement on globally accepted norms for economic actions and decisions—in short, for an ethic of doing business—is still in its infancy.

A global economic ethic—a common fundamental vision of what is legitimate, just, and fair—relies on moral principles and values that from time immemorial have been shared by all cultures and have been supported by common practical experience.

Each one of us—in our diverse roles as entrepreneurs, investors, creditors, workers, consumers, and members of different interest groups in all countries—bears a common and essential responsibility—together with our political institutions and international organizations—to recognize and apply this kind of global economic ethic.

For these reasons, the signatories of this declaration express their support of the following Manifesto.

Manifesto for a Global Economic Ethic

In this declaration, the fundamental principles and values of a global economy are set forth, according to the *Declaration toward a Global Ethic* issued by the Parliament of World Religions in Chicago in 1993. *The principles in this manifesto can be endorsed by all men and women with ethical convictions, whether these be religiously grounded or not.* The signatories of this declaration commit themselves to being led by its letter and its spirit in their day-to-day economic decisions, actions, and general behavior. This Manifesto for a Global Economic Ethic takes seriously the rules of the market and of competition; it intends to put these rules on a solid ethical basis for the welfare of all. Nothing less than the experience of the current crisis affecting the whole economic sphere underlines the need for those internationally accepted ethical principles and moral standards, which we all need to breathe life into in our daily business practices.

The principle of humanity

The ethical frame of reference: Differences between cultural traditions should not be an obstacle to engaging in active cooperation for esteem, defense, and fulfillment of human rights. Every human being—without distinction for age, sex, race, skin color, physical or mental ability, language, religion, political view, or national or social origin—possesses an inalienable and untouchable dignity. Everyone, the individual as well as the state, is therefore obliged to honor this dignity and protect it. Humans must always be the subjects of rights, must be ends and never mere means, and must never be the objects of commercialization and industrialization in economics, politics, and the media, in research institutes, or in industrial corporations.

The fundamental principle of a desirable global economic ethic is humanity. Being human must be the ethical yardstick for all economic action. It becomes concrete in the following guidelines for doing business in a way that creates value and is oriented to values for the common good.

Article 1

The ethical goal of sustainable economic action, as well as its social prerequisite, is the creation of a fundamental framework for sustainably fulfilling human beings' basic needs so that they can live in dignity. For that reason, in all economic decisions the uppermost precept should be that such actions always serve the formation and development of all the individual resources and capabilities that are needed for a truly human development of the individual and for living together happily.

Article 2

Humanity flourishes only in a culture of respect for the individual. The dignity and self-esteem of all human beings— be they superiors, coworkers, business partners, customers, or other interested persons—are inviolable. Never may human beings be treated badly, either through individual ways of conduct or through dishonorable trading or working conditions. The exploitation and the abuse of situations of dependence as well as the arbitrary discrimination of persons are irreconcilable with the principle of humanity.

Article 3

To promote good and avoid evil is a duty of all human beings. Thus this duty must be applied as a moral yardstick to all economic decisions and courses of action. It is legitimate to pursue one's own interests, but the deliberate pursuit of personal advantage to the detriment of one's partners—that is, with unethical means—is irreconcilable with sustainable economic activity to mutual advantage.

Article 4

What you do not wish done to yourself, do not do to others. This *Golden Rule* of reciprocity, which for thousands of years has been acknowledged in all religious and humanist traditions, promotes mutual responsibility, solidarity, fairness, tolerance, and respect for all persons involved.

Such attitudes or virtues are the basic pillars of a global economic ethos. Fairness in competition and cooperation for mutual benefit are fundamental principles of a sustainably developing global economy that is in conformity with the *Golden Rule*.

Basic values for global economic activity

The following basic values for doing business globally further develop the fundamental principle of humanity and make concrete suggestions for decisions, actions, and general behavior in the practical sphere of economic life.

Basic values: nonviolence and respect for life

The ethical frame of reference: To be authentically human in the spirit of our great religious and ethical traditions means that in public as well as in private life we must be concerned for others and ready to help. Every people, every race, and every religion must show tolerance and—indeed high appreciation—for every other—be they racial, ethnic, or religious—require protection and support by the majority.

Article 5
All human beings have the duty to respect the right to life and its development. Respect for human life is a particularly lofty good. Thus every form of violence or force in pursuit of economic goals is to be rejected. Slave labor, compulsory labor, child labor, corporal punishment, and other violations of recognized international norms of labor law must be suppressed and abolished. With utmost priority, all economic agents must guarantee the protection of human rights in their own organizations. At the same time, they must make every effort to see to it that, within their sphere of influence, they do nothing that might contribute to violations of human rights on the part of their business partners or other parties involved. In no way may they themselves draw profit from such violations.

The impairment of people's health through adverse working conditions must be stopped. Occupational safety and product safety according to state-of-the-art technology are basic rights in a culture of nonviolence and respect for life.

Article 6
Sustainable treatment of the natural environment on the part of all participants in economic life is an uppermost value-norm for

economic activity. The waste of natural resources and the pollution of the environment must be minimized by resource-conserving procedures and by environmentally friendly technologies. Sustainable clean energy (with renewable energy sources as far as possible), clean water, and clean air are elementary conditions for life. Every human being on this planet must have access to them.

Basic values: justice and solidarity

The ethical frame of reference: To be an authentic human being—in the spirit of the great religious and ethical traditions — not misusing economic and political power in a ruthless struggle for domination. Such power is instead to be used in the service of all human beings. Self-interest and competition serve the development of the productive capacity and the welfare of everyone involved in economic activity. Therefore, mutual respect, reasonable coordination of interests, and the will to conciliate and to show consideration must prevail.

Article 7

Justice and the rule of law constitute reciprocal presuppositions. Responsibility, rectitude, transparency, and fairness are fundamental values of economic life which must always be characterized by law-abiding integrity. All those engaged in economic activity are obliged to comply with the prevailing rules of national and international law. Where deficits exist in the quality or the enforcement of legal norms in a particular country, these should be overruled by self-commitment and self-control; under no circumstances may one take advantage of them for the sake of profit.

Article 8

The pursuit of profit is the presupposition for competitiveness. It is the presupposition for the survival of business enterprises and for their social and cultural engagements. Corruption inhibits the public welfare, damaging the economy and the people, because it systematically leads to false allocation and waste of resources. The suppression and abolition of corrupt and dishonest practices such as bribery, collusion agreements, patent piracy, and industrial espionage demands preventive engagement, which is a duty incumbent on all those active in the economy.

Article 9

A major goal of every social and economic system that aims at equal opportunity, distributive justice, and solidarity is to overcome hunger and ignorance, poverty and inequality, throughout the world. Self-help and outside help, subsidiarity and solidarity, private and public engagement—all these are two sides of the same coin: they become concrete in private and public economic investments, but also in private and public initiatives to create institutions that serve to educate all segments of the population and to erect a comprehensive system of social security. The basic goal of all such efforts is a true human development directed at the promotion of all those capabilities and resources that enable men and women to lead a life of self-determination in full human dignity.

Basic values: honesty and tolerance

The ethical frame of reference: To be authentically human in the spirit of our great religious and ethical traditions means that we must not confuse freedom with arbitrariness or pluralism with indifference to truth. We must cultivate integrity and truthfulness in all our relationships instead of dishonesty, dissembling, and opportunism.

Article 10

Truthfulness, honesty, and reliability are essential values for sustainable economic relationships that promote general human well-being. They are prerequisites for creating trust between human beings and for promoting fair economic competition. On the other hand, it is also imperative to protect the basic human rights of privacy and of personal and professional confidentiality.

Article 11

The diversity of cultural and political convictions, as well as the diverse abilities of individuals and the diverse competencies of organizations, represents a potential source of global prosperity. Cooperation for mutual advantage presupposes the acceptance of common values and norms and the readiness to learn from each other and to respectfully tolerate one another's otherness. Discrimination of human beings because of their sex, their race, their nationality, or their beliefs cannot be reconciled with the principles of a global economic ethic. Actions that do not respect or that violate the rights of other human beings are not to be tolerated.

Basic values: mutual esteem and partnership

The ethical frame of reference: To be authentically human in the spirit of our great religious and ethical traditions means the following: we need mutual respect, partnership, and under-standing instead of patriarchal domination and degradation, which are expressions of violence and engender counterviolence.

Every individual has intrinsic dignity and inalienable rights, and each also has an inescapable responsibility for what she or he does and does not do.

Article 12

Mutual esteem and partnership between all those involved—in particular, between men and women—is at once the prerequisite and the result of economic cooperation. Such esteem and partnership rest on respect, fairness, and sincerity toward one's partners, be they the executives of a firm or their employees, their customers, or other stakeholders. Esteem and partnership form the indispensable basis for recognizing situations in which unintentional negative consequences of economic actions pose a dilemma for all concerned—a dilemma that can and must be resolved by mutual effort.

Article 13

Partnership likewise finds its expression in the ability to participate in economic life, economic decisions, and economic gains. How such participation may be realized depends on the diverse cultural factors and regulatory structures prevailing in different economic areas. However, the right to join forces in order to responsibly pursue personal and group interests through collective action represents a minimal standard that must everywhere be recognized.

Conclusion

All economic agents should respect the internationally accepted rules of conduct in economic life; they should defend them and, within the framework of their sphere of influence, work together for their realization. Fundamental are the human rights and responsibilities as proclaimed by the United Nations in 1948.

Other global guidelines issued by recognized transnational institutions—the Global Compact of the United Nations, the Declaration on Fundamental Principles and Rights at Work of the International Labour Organization, the Rio Declaration on Environment and Development, and the UN Convention against Corruption, to name just a few—agree with the demands set forth in this Manifesto for a Global Economic Ethic.

Tübingen, 1 April 2009

First signatories

A.T. Ariyaratne, Founder-President,
Sarvodaya Movement, Sri Lanka
Leonardo Boff, Theologian and Writer, Brazil
Michel Camdessus,
Gouverneur honoraire de la Banque de France
Walter Fust, CEO, Global Humanitarian Forum
Prince El Hassan bin Talal, Jordan
Margot Kässmann,
Lutheran Bishop of Hanover and Chairperson of the Council of
the Evangelical Church in Germany
Georg Kell, Executive Director, UN Global Compact Office
Samuel Kobia,
General Secretary of World Council of Churches
Hans Küng, President, Global Ethic Foundation
Karl Lehmann, Cardinal, Bishop of Mainz
Klaus M. Leisinger, CEO, Novartis Foundation
Peter Maurer, Ambassador and Permanent
Representative of Switzerland to the United Nations
Mary Robinson, President, Realizing Rights:
The Ethical Globalization Initiative

Jeffrey Sachs, Director, The Earth Institute,
Columbia University
Juan Somavia, DirectorGeneral,
International Labour Organization
Desmond Tutu, Archbishop Emeritus
and Nobel Peace Prize Laureate
Daniel Vasella, CEO, Novartis International
Tu Weiming, Professor of Philosophy,
Harvard University and Beijing University
Patricia Werhane, Professor of Business Ethics, University of
Virginia, Darden School of Business and DePaul University
James D. Wolfensohn, former President of the World Bank
Carolyn Woo, Dean,
Mendoza College of Business University of Notre Dame

The Manifesto was composed by a working committee of the
Global Ethic Foundation:

Prof. Dr. Heinz-Dieter Assmann (Tübingen University)
Dr. Wolfram Freudenberg (Freudenberg Group)
Prof. Dr. Klaus Leisinger (Novartis Foundation)
Prof. Dr. Hermut Kormann (Voith AG)
Prof. Dr. Josef Wieland
(Drafter, Konstanz University of Applied Sciences)
Prof. H.C. Karl Schlecht (Putzmeister AG)

Officers of the Global Ethic Foundation:
Prof. Dr. Hans Küng (President)
Prof. Dr. Karl-Josef Kuschel (Academic Adviser)
Dr. Stephan Schlensog (Secretary-General)
Dr. Günther Gebhardt (Senior Adviser)

4. Blazing the Trail: "Yes to a Global Ethic" (1996)

(1) From the World of Politics and Culture

Richard v. Weizsäcker, former President of the Federal Republic of Germany, *Towards a Shared Global Ethic*. Advances and setbacks over security – Democracy lives by ethical presuppositions – A call to the religions.

Lew Kopelew, winner of the Peace Prize of the German Book Trade, *The Destiny of Humankind is at Stake*. History gives us examples – The necessary unity of science, politics and morality – What should govern world politics in the future.

Mary Robinson, President of the Republic of Ireland, *No Human Progress without a Global Ethic*. The imbalance between power and powerlessness, listening – sharing – collaboration.

Helmut Schmidt, former Chancellor of the Federal Republic of Germany, *Key Principles for a Humane Society*. Reflecting again on ethical principles – Do the religions have the power?

Martti Ahtisaari, President of the Republic of Finland, *Shared International Responsibility*. A Global Ethic furthers the aims of the Conference on European Security – Cultural and ethical values – Information as an ethical problem.

Cornelio Sommaruga, President of the International Committee of the Red Cross, *Indispensable for Survival*. In accord with the principles of the Red Cross – For the respecting of human dignity.

Juan Somavía, Chilean Ambassador at the United Nations, *An Inspiration for all of us.* The transforming power of the ethic – Putting principles into practice.

Rigoberta Menchú, Nobel Peace Prize winner, *My Irrevocable Creed.* Indispensable ingredients of peace – Commitment for Guatemala.

Carl Friedrich v. Weizsäcker, winner of the Peace Prize of the German Book Trade, *The Declaration on a Global Ethic.* Scientific experience – What ethical conclusions follow? – The role of ethics in religion – Incomplete religion.

Lord Yehudi Menuhin, musician, *My Prayer.*

(2) From the World of Judaism

Teddy Kollek, former Mayor of Jerusalem, *An Answer from Jerusalem on the Project of a Global Ethic.* One city, two peoples, three religions – The desire for an ethic out of the catastrophe – What is required of Jews? – Understanding between the religions is possible.

Rabbi Jonathan Magonet, Principal of Leo Baeck College, *Judaism and a Global Ethic.* The ambivalence of universalism – The biblical foundations of a global ethic – For the sake of peace.

Professor André Chouraqui, writer and translator, *Foundations for a Global Ethic according to the Bible, the Gospels and the Qur'an.* Global Ethic and covenant – The encounter of the Abrahamic religions – The hope for peace through the religions.

Sir Sigmund Sternberg, Chair of the Executive Committee of the International Council of Christians and Jews, *The World Seeks Moral and Spiritual Leadership*. Bringing together people of faith – Towards a "World Council of Faiths."

Elie Wiesel, Nobel Peace Prize winner, For an Ethic which Honours Humankind and the Creator.

René Samuel Sirat, Chief Rabbi of France, *Signs of Hope*. A letter about the global ethic.

(3) From the World of Christianity

Cardinal Franz König, former Archbishop of Vienna, *The Human Race as a Community of Destiny*. Putting a global ethic in the religious heritage of humankind – Peace, a task for the religions.

Konrad Raiser, General Secretary of the World Council of Churches, *Global Order and Global Ethic*. No human rights without a basic moral consensus – A new moral culture – What is the status and scope of a global ethic?

Patriarch Bartholomew I., Ecumenical Patriarch of Constantinople, *Reconciliation between the Nations and the Peace of the World*. Against the absolutizing of nationalism and racism – History is moved by the "power of weakness" – Approaching basic problems: unemployment and the destruction of the environment.

George Carey, Archbishop of Canterbury, *Tolerance and Integrity of One's Own Faith are not Mutually Exclusive*. Genuine tolerance should be based upon a true acceptance of one another. Proper understanding of the integrity and uniqueness of faith.

Cardinal Joseph Bernardin, Archbishop of Chicago, *In Agreement with Christianity*. An experiment – What is the basis for morality? – Can ethics exist apart from faith? – The need for systemic change – The four irrevocable directives.

Cardinal Paulo Evaristo Arns, Archbishop of Sao Paulo, *The Ethic of Peace*. What is peace? – The dedication of the religions to peace – Towards a just economic order – Local centres of human rights – Health and medical care.

Desmond Tutu, Anglican Archbishop of Capetown and Nobel Peace Prize winner, *Religion and Human Rights*. Every human being is an image of God – Human freedom and liberation – The positive influence of religion – Pathological aspects of religion.

(4) From the World of Islam

Crown Prince Hassan bin Talal, Crown Prince of the Hashemite Kingdom of Jordan, *Towards a New Way of Thinking*. The great challenges for humankind – All human beings are dependent on one another.

Muhammad El-Ghazali, Sheikh at the Al-Azhar University in Cairo, *Striving for a Higher Ethic*. Readiness for peace, and a proviso – The moral power of religion – The commandment of justice.

Hassan Hanafi, Professor of Philosophy in the University of Cairo, *The Religions Must Work Together*. Problems of practical application – The problem of minorities in the Islamic world – Unresolved questions of world politics and world justice.

Mahmoud Zakzouk, Dean of the Faculty of Islamic Theology in the Al-Azhar University of Cairo, *On Human Unity and Equality*, Humanity as God's governor – Acting with responsible awareness.

Muhammad Talbi, Professor of Islamic History at the University of Tunis, *A Charter of Duties and Tasks for All Human Beings*. Religion as a foundation for values – A worldwide process of growing awareness – Ethics for the religious and the nonreligious.

(5) From the World of the Eastern Religions

Hajime Nakamura, Professor in the University of Tokyo, *Thoughts on the Parliament of the World's Religions*. The one eternal religion in all religions – Buddhism gains new strength – Shinto becomes international – World peace through the discovery of the nature of religion.

Sulak Sivaraksa, Professor and civil rights leader, *As a Buddhist I support .... A letter in a difficult situation*.

L.M. Singhvi, High Commissioner of India for the United Kingdom, *The Charter of a Global Order*. A message.

Dileep Padgaonkar, Professor, *Redefining Tolerance*. The paradoxical situation of humankind – Strengthening common moral and spiritual values.

Shu-hsien Liu, Professor of Philosophy at the Chinese University in Hong Kong, *Global Ethic – A Confucian Response*. The great openness of Confucianism – The problem of human rights in Asia – Hope for a better world.

Aung San Suu Kyi, Nobel Peace Prize winner, *Towards a Culture of Peace and Development.* Human development is more than economic growth – Are democracy and human rights in contradiction with national culture? – Different peoples must agree on basic human values – Human beings must be rated higher than power – The challenge to ally oneself with human rights.

Count K. K. von der Groeben, On the Establishment of a Global Ethic Foundation.

5. A Global Ethic on the Global Agenda

Already five years after the publication of the Hans' book *Global Responsibility,* various commissions and institutions were voicing their demands for a global ethic at international conferences. The *Declaration Toward a Global Ethic* of the Parliament of the World's Religions and the proposal of the InterAction Council for a *Universal Declaration of Human Responsibilities,* also described here, were followed by a number of important statements, excerpts of which are given below (italics by H. K.):

(1) The UN Commission for Global Governance brought out a report on *Our Global Neighborhood* (1995). Chapter II, 3 calls for a global civic ethic:

"We therefore urge the international community to unite in support of a global ethic of common rights and shared responsibilities. In our view, such an ethic—reinforcing the fundamental rights that are already part of the fabric of international norms—would provide the moral foundation for constructing a more effective system of global governance." (Commission on Global Governance, *Our Global Neighborhood*).

(2) The World Commission on Culture and Development published a report on *Our Creative Diversity* (1995). Chapter I outlines the basis for a new global ethic:

"Cooperation between different people with different interests and from different cultures will be facilitated and conflict kept within acceptable and even constructive limits, if participants can see themselves as being bound and motivated by shared commitments. It is, therefore, imperative to look for a core of shared ethical values and principles. ... The idea is that the values and principles of a global ethic should be the shared points of reference, providing the minimal moral guidance the world must heed in its manifold efforts to tackle the global issues outlined above." (*Report of the World Commission on Culture and Development*, Our Creative Diversity).

(3) *Third Millennium Project of the City of Valencia* (in cooperation with UNESCO) presented a final report: *Proposals for Future Orientation and Activities* (1997). In conclusion number 15 it was stated:

"There can be no doubt that a global scenario, to say nothing of a new world order, requires the tacit or explicit acceptance of a number of global ethical principles. These principles must reflect a minimum of global values for societies and nations to be able to live together in harmony. We must take steps to ensure conditions in which tolerance can develop and different societies can coexist. There can be no survival of humanity without a coalition of believers and nonbelievers in an atmosphere of mutual respect. These principles can be supplemented by a Citizens' Charter and a charter on the rights and duties of nations."

(4) The 1997 World Economic Forum (Davos/Switzerland) also considered the problem. The press release of February 4 stated:

The World Economic Forum demands "the formulation of a declaration of human responsibilities with an international consensus about what these would consist of. 'The term fundamental human rights has been with us for some time, but there is no similarly broad understanding of fundamental human duties and responsibilities', said Klaus Schwab, founder and president of the Forum. 'But with increasing globalization, a constructive international dialogue about shared values and human responsibilities is a natural next step.' At the Forum's Annual Meeting, a group of well-known ethicists and legal scholars declared that the convergence of continued global violations of human rights with the forces of globalization calls for a new shared definition of ethical values and responsible human behavior."

(5) The UNESCO Universal Ethics Project 1997 (Paris) noted in its final recommendations:

"Moral values and ethical principles which could constitute the core of a universal ethic must be discovered and determined through reflection and empirically by identifying and reflecting on those values and principles which enjoy widespread recognition and/or which are rationally necessary. The project will take as its starting point the already existing efforts towards the formulation of universal rights values and norms."

(6) The 6th Indira Gandhi Conference in Delhi (1997) on *Post-colonial World: Interdependence and Identities* formulated in number 17 of its conclusions:

"In a globalizing world where a dramatic paradigm shift with regard to beliefs, attitudes and behaviors of societies and individuals is taking place, the time has come to work towards shared, universal ethical principles, on which all religions and cultures can agree. They can serve as a basis for the formulation of a more comprehensive set of human duties, obligations and standards, which would complement and correspond to the Universal Declaration of Human Rights. The 50th anniversary of the Declaration of Human Rights would be a suitable time for such an initiative." (Draft Conclusions: Sixth Indira Gandhi Conference: "Post-Colonial World: Interdependence and Identities").

(7) At the request of the Secretary-General of the United Nations Kofi Annan, a *Group of Eminent Persons* compiled the report, "Crossing the Divide" (2001), in which they stated:

"Reconciliation is the highest form of dialogue. It includes the capacity to listen, the capacity not only to convince but also to be convinced and most of all, the capacity to extend forgiveness. In essence, it is dialogue as a basis for the future, not dialogue as a recrimination for the past. ... It is reconciliation that may lead all of us, no matter how this reconciliation process is achieved, to discover and to establish a *global ethic*. A global ethic for institutions and civil society, for leaders and for followers, requires a longing and striving for peace, longing and striving for justice, longing and striving for partnerships, longing and striving for truth. These might be the four pillars of a system of a global ethic that reconciliation, as the new answer to the vicious circle of endless hatred, is going to provide us." ("Crossing the Divide. Dialogue among Civilizations"; www.uno.org).

How much better would the state of the world be in the third millennium, if all of these demands could be included in the global agenda and would be successively implemented!

(8) A global ethic from the point of view of Christian churches. The following excerpts clearly show that prominent representatives of Christian churches also argue in favor of a global ethic:

1. Meeting between Pope Benedict XVI and Professor Hans Küng

Press release

On Saturday, 24 September 2005, Pope Benedict XVI and Professor Hans Küng (Tübingen) met for a friendly conversation. Both sides agreed that for this conversation there was no point in entering into a dispute about those questions of Church teachings, which were the object of contention between Hans Küng and the Magisterium of the Catholic Church. For this reason, the conversation centered on two areas which in recent years have been at the forefront of Hans Küng's work: the question of a global ethic and the dialogue between the natural sciences and the Christian faith.

Professor Küng made it clear that the *Global Ethic Project* was not an abstract intellectual construct. On the contrary, the aim was to highlight those moral values on which the great religions of the world, despite all their differences, tended to converge and which, by reason of their convincing meaningfulness, had proved to be valid standards on which secular thinking could also agree. The Pope praised Professor Küng's efforts to contribute—through a dialogue with religions and with secular thinking—to a renewed recognition of the essential moral values of mankind. He emphasized that the engagement for a renewed awareness of the values underpinning human life was also an essential concern of his pontificate.

The Pope also praised Professor Küng's efforts to reinvigorate the dialogue between *faith and the natural sciences* and to bring to the fore the necessity and the reasonableness of posing the question regarding God in the context of scientific thinking. For his part, Professor Küng expressed his approval of the efforts of the Pope to promote a dialogue between the religions and the encounters with diverse social groups in the modern world.

Città del Vaticano, 26 September 2005

2. Bishop Dr. Margot Kässmann
Weimar Address (Weimar, 4 March 2007): "Religion as a factor which can deescalate conflicts"

"(...) The Catholic theologian and author Hans Küng once said: 'There can be no peace between nations without peace between the religions!' With his 'Global Ethic Project' he has tirelessly struggled to promote just such a peace. In the course of his studies and based on his experiences Hans Küng concluded that, despite all the differences between their beliefs, teachings, and rites, differences which should not be underestimated, nevertheless it was also possible to detect similarities, convergences, and correspondences between the world religions. Every human being is confronted by the same big questions, the age-old questions about where we and the world around us come from and where we are going, the question of how to deal with suffering and guilt, the question of the standards according to which we should live and act, the question of the purpose of life and death. All religions offer both a message of salvation and a path to salvation, all religions communicate a religious outlook

212

about life, a religious attitude towards life and a religious way of life; despite all their dogmatic differences they also communicate certain shared ethical standards.

For Küng, these observations coalesced in the 1990s into a central question: What is this shared basic ethic? In 1988 Küng had written: 'our ethical interrelatedness could become a unifying bond to promote peace between the community of nations, could contribute to a more free, a more just, a more peaceful coexistence in a world which is becoming increasingly uninhabitable.' Taking this as his starting point, Küng coined the term 'global ethic' in analogy to global politics, the global economy, the global financial system. A global ethic should not be understood as a compellingly Christian ethic but as an ethic in a new interreligious and intercultural sense. Believers from all religions and nonbelievers from all cultures can find something they collectively share. These are basic ethical standards which can be affirmed by all.

A humane ethic has two basic principles: every person should be treated humanely and not inhumanely, and the so-called Golden Rule: do not do unto others that which you do not wish them to do unto you, or, in the biblical version: 'In everything, therefore, treat the people the same way you want them to treat you!' (Mt 7:12). Küng lists four immoveable directives on which the great religious and philosophical traditions agree:

1. Have respect for life. This is the ancient commandment: You shall not kill, understood in our times as a commitment to a culture of nonviolence and respect for life.

2. Act honestly and fairly. This is the ancient commandment: You shall not steal, understood in our times as a commitment to a culture of solidarity and a just economic order.

3. Talk and act truthfully. This is the ancient commandment: You shall not lie, understood in our times as a commitment to a culture of tolerance and a life of truthfulness.

4. Respect and love one another. This is the ancient commandment: You shall not abuse sexuality, understood in our times as a commitment to a culture of equality and partnership between men and women.

The Global Ethic Project aims at a global understanding between the religions with the goal of a common ethic for humanity, but one which is not intended as a replacement for religion. An ethic is and remains, according to Küng, only one dimension of a religion and between religions. The goal is not a single uniform religion, not a cocktail of religions or the substitution of religion by an ethic. That point is important for me, as I have no very high opinion of 'a mishmash of religions'.

The Global Ethic Project is an attempt to promote the urgently required peace between people from the different religions of this world. Hans Küng summarized his vision in four sentences: 'No peace among nations without peace between the religions, no peace between the religions without a dialogue between the religions, no dialogue between the religions without global ethical standards, no survival on Earth without a universal ethic, a global ethic.'

(…) Trust develops through holding a dialogue with one another, through encounters between religions. In the shared will to

214

contribute to de-escalating the current situation, the Global Ethic Project has much to offer. It is not necessary to continually invent things anew. What is particularly important is that religions do not demonize each other, that they are aware of fundamentalism in their own ranks, that they always espouse the freedom of others and resolutely reject every form of violence, branding it a form of blasphemy. That is what I expect from the adherents of every religion."

Bibliography

Annan, Kofi, Do We Still Have Common Values?, 3rd Global Ethic Lecture, Tübingen, 2003, www.weltethos.org.

Behr, Benita von–Zillinger, Martin (Ed.), Global Ethic. A Guideline for Economy and Politics. International Conference for Students. Documentation, Tübingen, 1997.

Blair, Tony, Global Politics and Global Ethic, 1st Global Ethic Lecture, Tübingen, 2000, www.weltethos.org.

Braybrooke, Marcus (Ed.), Stepping Stones to a Global Ethic, London, 1992.

A Call to our Guiding Institutions. Council for the Parliament of the World's Religions. Presented on the Occasion of the 1999 Parliament of the World's Religions in Cape Town, South Africa: www.cpwr.org.

Czada, Roland; Held, Thomas; Weingardt, Markus (eds.), Religions and World Peace, Baden-Baden, Nomos, 2012.

Dierksmeier, Claus u.a., Humanistic Ethics in the Age of Globality, Houndmills, Basingstoke, 2011.

Dierksmeier, Claus, How Should we do Business? Global Ethics in the Age of Globality, 10th Global Ethic Lecture, Tübingen, 2012, www.weltethos.org.

Dierksmeier, Claus, Reframing Economic Ethics. The Philosophical Foundations of Humanistic Management. Palgrave Macmillan, London/New York, 2016.

Dunning, John H. (Hrsg.), Making Globalization Good. The Moral Challenges of Global Capitalism, New York, 2003.

Ebadi, Shirin, The contribution of Islam to a Global Ethic, 5th Global Ethic Lecture, Tübingen, 2004, www.weltethos.org.

Fraser, Malcolm – Fukuda, Yasuo – Rosen, Jeremy (eds.), Interfaith Dialogue. Ethics in Decision-Making, InterAction Council, Tokyo, 2015.

Freedman, Benedict, Rescuing the Future, 2010.

Global Ethic and Globalization Teaching Kit (including CD-ROM), The Hong Kong Institute of Education and The Centre for Religious and Spirituality Education, Hong Kong, 2011.

Green, Stephen K., Global Economy – Global Ethic, 9th Global Ethic Lecture, Tübingen 2010, www.weltethos.org.

H. Küng, K. M. Leisinger, J. Wieland, Manifesto Global Economic Ethic. Consequences and Challenges for Global Businesses (dtv, München 2010).

Ka, Lok Tsang (ed.) Global Ethic and Globalization. Collections for General Education, Roundtable Synergy Books, Hong Kong, 2014.

Keir, Jonathan, From Global Ethic to World Ethos? Building on Hans Küng's Legacy of Basic Trust in Life, Karls Schlecht Stiftung (KSG), Aichtal, 2018.

Köhler, Horst, Why Should Others Concern Us?, 4th Global Ethic Lecture, Tübingen 2004, www.weltethos.org.

Küng, Hans – Kuschel, Karl-Josef (Ed.), A Global Ethic. The Declaration of the Parliament of World's Religions, London 1993; New York 1993.

Küng, Hans – Schmidt, Helmut (Ed.), A Global Ethic and Global Responsibilities. Two Declarations, London 1998; New York 1999.

Küng, Hans (Ed.), Yes to a Global Ethic, New York 1996; London, 1996.

Küng, Hans (together with Walter Homolka) How to Do Good & Avoid Evil. A Global Ethic from the Sources of Judaism, SkyLight Paths, Woodstock/Vermont, 2009.

Küng, Hans, A Global Ethic for Global Politics and Economics, London 1997; New York 1998.

Küng, Hans, Disputed Truth. Memoirs II, Continuum, London, 2008.

Küng, Hans, Global Responsibility. In Search of a New World Ethic, New York 1991; London 1991.

Küng, Hans, Islam. Past, Present & Future, Oneworld, Oxford 2007; The American University in Cairo Press, Kairo, 2007.

Küng, Hans, Judaism. The Religious Situation of Our Time, London, 1992; also as: Judaism. Between Yesterday and Tomorrow, New York, 1992.

Küng, Hans, My Struggle for Freedom. Memoirs, Eerdmans, Grand Rapids, Mich., 2003; Novalis, Ottawa 2003; Continuum, London 2003.

Küng, Hans, The Beginning of All Things. Science and Religion, Eerdmans, Grand Rapids, Michigan, 2007.

Küng, Hans, Tracing the Way. Spiritual Dimensions of the World Religions, London 2002; New York 2002.

Küng, Hans, What I believe (Continuum, London, 2010).

Kuokkanen, Aleksi, Constructing Ethical Patterns in Times of Globalization. Hans Küng's Global Ethic Project and Beyond, (Faculty of Theology) University of Helsinki, Helsinki 2010; Leiden 2012.

Kuschel, Karl-Josef, Abraham. A Symbol of Hope for Jews, Christians and Muslims, London, 1995.

Okeja, Uchenna B., Normative Justification of a Global Ethic: A Perspective from African Philosophy, Lanham/Maryland: Lexington Books, 2013. 2013.

Our Global Neighbourhood. The Commission on Global Governance, Oxford, 1995.

Picco, Giandomenico; Aboulmagd, Kamal A.; Küng, Hans (et al.), Crossing the Divide. Dialogue among Civilizations, South Orange, NJ, 2001.

Robinson, Mary, Ethics, Human Rights and Globalization, 2nd Global Ethic Lecture, Tübingen 2002, www.weltethos.org.

Rogge, Jacques, Global Sport and Global Ethic, 6th Global Ethic Lecture, Tübingen, 2006, www.weltethos.org.

Schmidt, Helmut, On a politician's ethics, 7th Global Ethic Lecture, Tübingen, 2007, www.weltethos.org.

Shingleton, Bradley – Stilz, Eberhard (eds.), The Global Ethic and Law: Intersections and Interactions, Baden-Baden, 2015.

Tutu, Desmond, Global Ethic and Human Dignity: an African Perspective, 8th Global Ethic Lecture, Tübingen, 2009, www.weltethos.org.

WELTETHOS – A Vision in Music, City of Birmingham Symphony Orchestra (cbso), booklet, season 2011–12.

World Religions – Universal Peace – Global Ethic, ed. by Global Ethic Foundation, Tübingen, 2000.

Zhang Hua, A Reader of Global Ethics (chin.), Shandong University Press, Hong Kong.

Zhang, Sheng Yu, A Study of Hans Küng's Way From Theology to Global Ethics (chin.) (Licentiate-Thesis, Fujen Catholic University), Taipei Hsien, 2001.

For further information about the Global Ethic Foundation and its work see:
www.weltethos.org
www.global-ethic.org
www.facebook.com/stiftungweltethos